MW00682597

Getting
Your
Life
Out
of
Neutral

Other Books by Gary R. Collins

How to Be a People Helper

The Rebuilding of Psychology

You Can Profit From Stress

Christian Counseling: A Comprehensive Guide

Helping People Grow

Give Me a Break: The How-to-Handle-Pressure Book for Teens

Calm Down

Beyond Easy Believism

Getting Started

The Sixty-Second Christian

The Magnificant Mind

Innovative Approaches to Counseling

Getting
Your
Life
Out
of
Neutral

Gary R. Collins, Ph. D.

Fleming H. Revell Company
Old Tappan, New Jersey

Unless otherwise identified, Scripture quotations in this book are taken from the HOLY BIBLE: NEW INTERNATIONAL VERSION. Copyright © 1973, 1978 by the International Bible Society. Used by permission of Zondervan Bible Publishers.

Verses marked TLB are taken from The Living Bible, Copyright © 1971 by Tyndale House Publishers, Wheaton, Ill. Used by permission.

Verse marked KJV is taken from the King James Version of the Bible.

Adapted excerpts, under "Values," p. 266, from PEAK PERFORMERS: The New Heroes of American Business, by Charles Garfield. Copyright © 1986 by Garfield Enterprises, Inc. Used by permission of William Morrow & Company, Inc.

"Quotes from *Twelve Ways to Develop a Positive Attitude* by Dale E. Galloway, copyright © 1975, are used by permission of Tyndale House Publishers, Inc.

Library of Congress Cataloging-in-Publication Data

Collins, Gary R.
    Getting your life out of nutral.

    Bibliography: p.
    Includes index.
    1. Christian life—1960–   . 2. Life skills.
I. Title.
BV4501.2.C6435   1987   248.4   87-4341
ISBN 0-8007-1531-4

All rights reserved. No part of this publication may be reproduced, stored in a retrieval system, or transmitted in any form or by any means—electronic, mechanical, photocopy, recording, or any other—except for brief quotations in printed reviews, without the prior permission of the publisher.

Copyright © 1987 by Gary R. Collins

Published by the Fleming H. Revell Company
Old Tappan, New Jersey 07675
Printed in the United States of America

Contents

Foreword

Is your life in neutral?

I had a car with a bad transmission once. It kept getting stuck in park and would slip from drive into neutral at the worst possible times! Just when I was trying to move into the passing lane, for example.

Now if you have a life like that, you better do what I did—get yourself to a transmission expert.

Dr. Gary Collins is a life-transmission expert!

Are you stuck in a job or a relationship that's going nowhere? Are you about to give up on a marriage that's slipped into neutral? You need a serious overhaul, my friend, because life is fantastic . . . and in case no one ever told you, you're the only one who can live it.

During my twenty years as president of the Fortune Group my team and I have been helping companies succeed by showing managers how to manage. Everyone has mana-

gerial problems. The real problem is that everyone thinks
they know how to manage, just like everyone thinks they
know how to live. But not everyone knows how to *really*
manage or *really* live.

You get in a rut.

You travel the same highways to and from work every
day . . . and you travel the same thoughtways once you get
there.

You slip into neutral.

Yet you've got an overdrive potential you've only dreamt
of . . . so Gary Collins has designed this self-instruction
manual on how you can get yourself purring like a fine-
tuned race car.

Dr. Collins, if he were here, would step in right
about now and start qualifying my claims for him. "No, I'm
just a well-trained mechanic; I can show you how it ought to
work, but the rest is up to you."

Right on doctor! Show me! And then let me live. The
point is this man has seen it all as a teacher, counselor, and
speaker to groups and individuals around the world. He's
worked with college students who were so smart they knew
everything, and American servicemen some of whom were
so sad they didn't think they knew anything, and then he's
worked with the likes of you and me who sometimes don't
know if we're coming, going . . . or need an oil change. You
see, this book has been *road tested*. This is not some therapy
theory that Dr. Ivory Tower dreamed up. This is real stuff,
where the rubber meets the road . . . just look at the skid
marks in some of the life stories here and you'll see. And
you can be sure the information is good, because Dr. Collins is an honest-to-goodness Ph.D. and not the kind that
popped up out of a hot tub in California.

And he's going to challenge you to look at your whole
life. Not just this piece or that part. Not just your professional life, but your social life, your love life, your spiritual

life. And to encourage you, you're going to hear about real people who did marvelous things . . . not just the usual list of "success stories" but the honest stories of pious, poor, simple, generous, and renewed people who became extraordinary because they discovered down deep they were made for more than coasting.

When you get yourself out of neutral, you come and see me at the Fortune Group and I'll show you how to be a financial success . . . but don't bother to come until you've got your priorities straight and your gears working right and have been fully checked out through Dr. Collins's marvelous new book.

W. Steven Brown
President of the Fortune Group
Author of *Thirteen Fatal Errors Managers Make . . . and How You Can Avoid Them.*

Getting
Your
Life
Out
of
Neutral

One

Managing
Your
Life

Ricky Hosea was ready to leave.

The limousine had arrived. The rented video camera was ready. The hospital staff, many fighting back tears, were clustered near the doorway.

Shortly after noon, Ricky rose slowly from his wheelchair and grabbed the two canes that steady and help keep his twenty-three-year-old body erect. He paused for a minute before pushing the revolving door. Then, while the video camera recorded his triumph, Ricky Hosea walked through the cold winter air to take his place in the backseat of the waiting limousine.

It had been a long two years since that night when Ricky was struck as he walked along Highway A1A in Key West. The car that flipped him in the air sped away and another, in the hands of a drunken sailor, left Ricky's body mangled and broken. He was not expected to live.

But Ricky Hosea had other plans. When he was brought, several months later, to the Rehabilitation Institute of Chicago, the young patient told a nurse about his goal. "When I leave here," he said, "I am not going out in a wheelchair. I'm going to walk out through those revolving doors."

Everybody knew that wouldn't be easy. Ricky's wife had already given up. While he was still paralyzed from the waist down she filed for divorce. "I don't want to be married to only half a man," she told her bedridden husband. The doctors who performed several dozen operations had trouble believing Ricky would walk again. The nurses were equally skeptical. But after weeks of pain and frustration, months of paralysis, countless hours of physical therapy, long periods of discouragement, and massive doses of persistence and determination, Ricky left the hospital—walking.

He determined to go in style. So he ordered a custom-made three-piece suit to clothe his battered but healing body, sent flowers and a touching thank-you note to the hospital staff, then walked through that revolving door, out to the limousine, and into a new life.[1]

Life Management

How will Ricky Hosea manage life now that he is on his own? How will he handle his feelings, his relationships with other people, his money, his career, his stresses, his values, his attitudes, his religious beliefs, his dreams? After this long hospitalization, how will he get his life going again. How will he get it out of neutral?

People like Ricky—and the rest of us—have no difficulty finding advice on issues like these. It flows freely from the pages of self-help books or the speakers at management seminars. Some of the guidance isn't very helpful, but much is attractively packaged, clearly presented, and of genuine value.

Why, then, do people still struggle in spite of all the self-help resources? Why do we have insecurities, discouragement, questions about the future, problems in managing time or money, anxiety, worries about our careers, marital tensions, and a host of other life-management problems?

Managing our lives involves more than reading a self-help book or sitting through a seminar. It is not enough to gather advice and accumulate information. We need to apply our knowledge to real-life situations. We must learn skills and take actions that enable us to cope with the unexpected.

Not long ago I was stranded unexpectedly in a Central American airport. I had spent two busy weeks on a speaking trip to Honduras and was looking forward to my return home. It came as no surprise when the plane was late, but after two or three hours I was disturbed to hear talk about our leaving mañana.

Terry—he told everybody his name—heard the talk too, and he didn't like it. Loud and insensitive, he was the typical "ugly American." His dress was sloppy. His demands were vehement. His criticisms were impassioned, especially when the cashier couldn't change the American hundred-dollar bill he was waving. The gracious and easygoing airport officials largely ignored him. Embarrassed North Americans, like me, cringed in the corners, hoping no one would identify us with our loud-talking countryman.

Apparently my fellow passenger had not learned that in this life we have to be flexible. We can't let circumstances and bitterness control us. In the midst of stressful situations, it helps to look for the positive and find things for which we can be thankful. When we are rigid, negative, and without gratitude, like Terry in that airport, life will defeat us and leave us perpetually frustrated.

How do we avoid this defeat and frustration? How can we manage ourselves more effectively?

Each of the following chapters contains five Life Management Principles. They are set in a box like the one below. Most are simple, well-known, and easily forgotten when life gets tough. They are practical principles: guidelines that work. They are the long-proven practices that have helped people like Ricky Hosea rise above life's frustrations and climb back from the point of death. They are conclusions that could help people like Terry in Honduras who couldn't even handle a change in his travel plans without making a fool of himself and his fellow travelers.

Everybody Has Problems

We have the strange view in this country that life should be easy.

M. Scott Peck is a psychiatrist who started a best-selling book with three little words: Life is difficult.[2] That, wrote Peck, is a great truth that most of us don't want to accept. We develop the habit of moaning about our problems, assuming that our burdens are unique, and acting as if life ought to be easy.

But life *isn't* easy. Often it isn't fair, and few people find much fun in squarely facing and solving problems. The past few years have not been easy for Ricky Hosea, but everybody knows he is a better man because of his determined efforts to walk again. His life is dramatic evidence that real personal growth comes only to those who face and overcome life's difficulties—even when this isn't easy.

If you're like me, you don't like that message. Most of us prefer, instead, to escape from problems, to avoid them, to ignore them, to pretend they will go away. When they don't disappear, we get angry and start complaining. We wait for someone else to do something or we talk ourselves into believing that stronger faith or a positive mental attitude will dissolve all our stresses.

One of my friends recently retired and set out, with his wife, on a lengthy trip in their new mobile home. They had plans for finding some ideal location to build a little dream house. They looked forward to spending their remaining years in a warm, sunny climate, giving themselves enthusiastically to their hobbies, and doting over their grandchildren.

One week after the long-anticipated retirement trip began, all of these careful plans collapsed abruptly. My friend had a stroke that took his life within forty-eight hours.

His wife was devastated in her grief but she had learned some important lessons many years earlier. She knew that everybody has pressures and problems. She realized that the difficulties of life never stop; growth and mental stability don't come to those who ignore problems. Like Ricky Hosea, my friend's wife realized that effective life management comes when we face difficulties honestly and take responsibility for solving problems or adapting to trying circumstances.

Problems Can Be Understood

Sometimes it doesn't take long for me to write a book, but before one word goes on the paper I usually have spent months and sometimes years reading and doing background research. In preparing this book, for example, I discovered a variety of authors who had written about life management.[3] Some of their books are scholarly, hard to read, and dull. Almost all suggest, however, that problems are understood, and solved, when they are seen from two viewpoints.

The Outside View: Circumstances

Many of life's problems come from sources that are largely beyond our control. The unexpected heart attack or accident, the government policies or economic trends that cause us to be fired, the new neighbors whose loud parties disrupt the peace and keep us awake at night, the severe storm that disrupts power and hinders travel, the child who is born brain-damaged or physically retarded—events like these are beyond our control and they often disrupt our lives radically.

From this it does not follow that we are no more than passive victims, pushed about by the vicissitudes of life. Even when pressures come from without, we can make choices. We can change our attitudes and ways of thinking. We can take actions that enable us to rise above even the greatest stresses of life.

This does not mean that we ignore the environment in which we live or work. Recently a sports complex closed, much to the consternation of local merchants who earned their living selling food, drinks, and souvenirs to visiting sports fans. No amount of wishful thinking, attitude change, or wallowing in despondency can alter the circumstances for those business people. The stadium is being torn down and the fans now go elsewhere. To accept this reality is a first step in recovering from the financial setbacks.

The Inside View: Attitudes

Too often, we forget that many pressures and problems arise or are made worse because of our thinking. People often do poorly as life managers because of internal self-defeating thoughts, fears, and attitudes.

There are times, for example, when most of us feel insecure. What if I'm not accepted? we wonder. What if my business fails? What will I do if I can't pass the exam? How do other people see me? Where do I fit in this world? What is my purpose in life? Where am I going? How can I cope with my present stresses? These are profoundly disturbing questions (many will be considered later) that can leave us feeling inadequate, frustrated, and immobilized.

At times we can also feel lonely, helpless, and confused. I once arrived, by myself, at the train station in Ankara, Turkey. Imagine how I felt when nobody was there to meet me as I had expected. I had no Turkish money, didn't speak the language, and had no idea how to contact the one person I knew in the country. Inner panic accomplishes nothing in such situations. I needed to find some kind stranger who could speak English to help me find a money exchange and start the search for my friend who had misplaced the note with my arrival time.

Internal self-defeating thoughts are not limited to unexpected situations like my experience in Ankara. At times all of us are bothered by inner insecurities and ongoing concerns about our private worries. Some people have difficulty controlling their drinking, temper outbursts, cynical comments, sexual lusts, persisting anxieties, lingering depression, or feelings of incompetence and failure. When there are inner struggles over these and similar issues, it is difficult to concentrate on other things. As a result, it is hard to manage life effectively.

Acceptance

Psychologist Gary Emery has proposed a three-step formula for handling life pressures. He calls the formula ACT: Accept reality, Choose to be independent, and Take action.[4]

The first of these steps, *acceptance,* goes beyond understanding a problem. Acceptance means that you are clearly aware of reality. It involves letting go of unrealistic fantasies, complaints, and demands that life should be different. It is a willingness to acknowledge and accommodate yourself to change. It involves making choices and taking responsibility for doing things differently.

Most of us find it easier to slip into one or more of the stages of nonacceptance:

- Nonawareness—"Don't tell me; I don't want to know."
- Disbelief—"I know but I can't believe it."
- Anger—"I'm mad that it happened."
- Depression—"It's terrible; things are so bad."
- Anxiety—"What will happen to me now?"[5]

Acceptance gets us to the point of saying, "What has happened, has happened, and I am willing to do what I can to adjust accordingly."

Problems Can Be Managed

Probably most of us admire political activists, especially when their actions bring reform and change for the better. England's William Wilberforce was such a man. Despite incredible opposition, he led the fight to abolish slave trading almost two hundred years ago. Ridiculed by critics, lampooned in popular cartoons, threatened by opponents, and sometimes discouraged almost to the point of quitting, Wilberforce nevertheless persisted and changed the course of history.

Some self-management books tell us to do the same. Set a clear goal, they suggest, refuse to quit, and keep on pushing until you get what you want. Such advice is inspiring but it isn't always realistic. Wilberforce was able to alter British law, but many life situations cannot be changed no matter how hard we try or how much we persist. The successful self-manager looks for and sometimes makes opportunities to change the world. More often, however, self-management involves changing ourselves—our thinking, our attitudes, our perceptions, our feelings, our actions.

Gordon MacDonald is a successful people manager who believes we must see ourselves as living in two different worlds.[6] The outer world is visible, easiest to deal with, and often mentioned in self-help books. It is the world of work, money management, success, schedules, family life, and social relationships.

It takes time and energy to manage the outer world, but plenty of help is available. This is a world addressed by management seminars, continuing education, strategy meetings, careful planning, practical books or articles, and some insightful sermons. Everybody can see this outer world. It cannot be ignored; it has to be heeded and controlled.

In contrast, the inner world is a quiet place of reflection on values, attitudes, beliefs, and spiritual issues that are less visible but still of crucial importance in life. This is a world where society's pressures, moral pollution, injustice, and cutthroat competition do not need to penetrate. For many, it is also a world that gets neglected and pushed aside while we tackle more prominent pressing issues. When this happens, the inner world never gets strong enough to sustain us through the real trials of life.

Howard Rutledge was an air force pilot, shot down over North Vietnam during the early months of the war. For several years he remained captive in an isolated environment with frequent beatings, deteriorating health, and hostile interrogations. Prior to his imprisonment, Rutledge had managed his outer world with precision. He had rarely joined his family in church, however, and was "too busy, too preoccupied, to spend one or two short hours a week thinking about the really important things." When he was captured, his previously neglected inner world had left him with few personal resources that could sustain and strengthen him through the long, lonely, pressure-filled months of confinement.[7] Following his release, Rutledge returned to freedom and determined never again to let the outer world's demands snuff out the inner spiritual dimension of his life.

Four A's

As a starting point for managing your outer and inner worlds it can be helpful to remember four words, all starting with the letter *A*.

First, *admit* the existence of problems and pressures when they arise. Life problems that aren't acknowledged may be forgotten for a while, but they don't get solved and they rarely go away by themselves.

Second, *analyze* what is causing the problem. Sometimes you can't see this clearly by yourself, so you may need the help and viewpoint of a perceptive friend. It is difficult to resolve a problem if we can't uncover and do something about the underlying cause.

Next, *accept* the things that cannot be changed. Even people with no interest in religion have been inspired by what has come to be known as the Alcoholics Anonymous prayer: God grant me the serenity to accept the things I cannot change, courage to change the things I can, and wisdom to know the difference.[8] Acceptance, as we have seen, is a basic part of life management.

Finally, *act* on what can be changed. This may involve changing circumstances that can be altered, but also changing the inner world of attitudes, thinking, and emotion.

While Terry was stomping around that Central American airport demanding the transportation that would not come until later, I tried (successfully) to apply these four *A*'s to myself. I admitted that no planes would be leaving at least until the next day, analyzed my feelings of disappointment and frustration, accepted the fact that nothing could be done to change the situation, and took action to call my wife, get hotel accommodations (at airline expense), and settle down to read one of the extra books that usually accompany me on trips, just in case I encounter unanticipated delays.

Locus of Control

Life problems are difficult to manage when we feel out of control. Maybe you have never been stranded in a foreign country, but have you ever been hospitalized? This can be a stressful experience, often because the patient feels so powerless. Hospitalization puts us into unfamiliar territory, under the control of doctors and nurses who may fail to explain what is happening or what to expect next.

Does it surprise you to know that there are individual differences in the extent to which we feel in control of life? Psychologists call this *locus of control.*

Some of us believe that life events usually come from chance or from the actions of other people. This viewpoint is called an *external* locus of control. It is a view that looks to others to help with the management of problems.

In contrast, others have an *internal* locus of control. They believe people more often cause their own problems and need to take responsibility for finding solutions.

Before reading further, you may want to take the test that appears at the end of this chapter. It will give some indication of your own locus of control.

It probably will come as no surprise for you to learn that the best self-managers are people who have an internal locus of control.[9] Probably they would agree with Shakespeare's words in *Julius Caesar:*

> Men at some time are masters of their fates;
> The fault, dear Brutus, is not in our stars,
> But in ourselves. . . .

Is it possible to change one's locus of control? Can people who score low on the internal scale become effective life managers? The answer, it appears, is yes. Change does not come quickly, but it can come. After you finish reading this book, perhaps you would like to take the locus of control test again to see if there are any changes in you.

Many Problems Can Be Prevented

Tom Peters attracted a lot of attention when he coauthored two highly acclaimed books on excellence.[10] With his colleagues, Peters analyzed America's best-run companies and tried to determine why they were successful.

Most of the findings were widely applauded, but many readers reacted to Peters's controversial conclusion about the price of success. No person can have both a full, satisfying personal life and a full, satisfying professional life, he wrote.[11] People who spend time growing roses, playing with the children, and interacting with the neighbors may be well liked, but they are never nominated for Nobel prizes, never win Olympic medals, never build big businesses, never reach the top of their fields. "The truth is that I simply have not seen many 'balanced' people soar to the heights, nice as the idea may be," Peters wrote. Some people think their lives are balanced, but their families or employers often think otherwise.

I don't like this conclusion, but I suspect it is largely true. It isn't easy to succeed simultaneously in all areas: in business, in work, in sports, in family relationships. It is difficult to keep things in balance and prevent problems from creeping into the various areas of life.

Even so, problems can be prevented. Some things can be done to keep our lives in balance and to stop existing problems from getting worse.

Plan Ahead

When I was on the trip that took me to Ankara, I gave a talk on stress to a group of military people stationed in eastern Turkey. Many were enjoying their tour of duty, but others were having difficulty adjusting to life in the Turkish culture. Why?

Some had come to Turkey with a clear understanding of what they would encounter. Before arriving, they knew that life would be different. They had heard that toilets, electrical outlets and voltage, food, and local values were different from those in America. They also knew that the people would be exceptionally friendly and that the country has a number of fascinating, relatively inexpensive vacation spots. Before arriving, these military people had planned ahead. They knew the potential problems and they had learned from others about ways to cope.

In contrast, many nonadjusters were surprised to find that their electrical appliances couldn't be used, their Turkish apartments were not air-conditioned, and their living accommodations were not as comfortable as those at home. These people were miserable because they had not planned ahead. Often they fell into the mind-set of ignoring the positive and dwelling on all the things about Turkey that were negative.

The old Boy Scouts' motto, Be Prepared, applies to most parts of life. Thinking ahead and planning accordingly can help us avoid problems, especially in new situations. There is increasing evidence that mental health improves and problems are prevented when people prepare for the future by becoming more knowledgeable and developing personal competence and greater social skills.[12] All of this involves getting more information and planning ahead.

Keep Things in Perspective

At some time all of us have been evaluated by psychological tests, school examinations, or employer evaluations. Most people overlook the positive things that come from these tests and dwell on the negative. I can have an entire class of students make positive comments about some course, but I go away remembering the one person who didn't like how I conducted the class.

It is easy to accentuate the negative, overlook the positive, and focus on what is pessimistic. Quickly such thinking drags us into discouragement and inactivity. When new problems arise, we can't cope because we have allowed things to get out of perspective. Negative thinking has taken control.

I have a friend whose life circumstances are often overwhelming. This lady does not deny her problems, but she tries to focus her mind on other things whenever she feels the subtle influence of self-pity creeping into her thinking. Periodically, she makes a list of the good and bad things in her life. This helps her keep things in perspective.

It helps, too, to get the viewpoint of someone who understands but is less involved emotionally. By getting a more balanced and less biased perspective we cope better and keep problems from getting worse.

The Double Win

Psychologist Denis Waitley has told the story of the Mahre twins, Steve and Phil, who represented the United States in the ski competition at the 1984 Olympic Winter Games. Born only minutes apart, the brothers had always been intense competitors. At last they were ready to compete for the ultimate athletic glory.

Phil went first. Cutting through the cold, biting wind, he tore down Bjelasnica Mountain with a speed that bettered the times of all the previous competitors. A gold medal was in sight.

But Steve was still at the mountaintop, waiting his turn to descend the slippery slope. Were people surprised when his brother called from a walkie-talkie in the valley and radioed advice? "Ski a straight course," Phil suggested. "Watch out for the bottom; it's slick."

When his turn came, Steve made some mistakes. His skis got locked and he wasn't fast enough to beat Phil's record. Steve got a silver medal; Phil got the gold—but the brothers illustrated a basic principle of life management.

Waitley calls it "the double win."[13] It goes against the old "If I win, you lose," philosophy. It rejects the view that we win through intimidation and by "looking out for number one." The double-win perspective says, "If I help you win, I win too." It assumes that the best way for me to win is to help you win as well. This is a giving perspective that works at home, in the business world, and even in the competitive world of sports. It is a philosophy that Steve and Phil Mahre demonstrated dramatically on that steep and icy slalom run in a remote and bleak corner of Yugoslavia.

Does the double win help prevent problems? Life is stressful for people who are always insecure, worried about being number one, afraid of losing their jobs, driving themselves to keep ahead of the competition. The win-win philosophy doesn't advocate laziness or a retreat from excellence. It encourages planning, goal setting, striving, determination. It also encourages sharing, caring, giving, and receiving. That is less stressful and far more fulfilling than the old win-lose idea. The double win assumes that we get the most out of life when we give our best to others. That attitude prevents life problems that could destroy us otherwise.

Life Management Involves Making Choices

Life is full of choices.

We can deny this or wish it weren't so. We can blame others for our problems, let somebody else make the hard decisions, or assume that our lives are controlled by luck or fate. Nevertheless the fact remains: Life is a series of choices.

You can choose to look at life from a negative perspective, or you can decide to be more positive.

You can choose to change your behavior, thinking, attitudes, beliefs, and morals, or you can decide to stay as you are.

You can choose to go through life dependent on the opinions and actions of others, or you can choose to make decisions that let you be independent and wholesomely interdependent.

You can choose to take action even when you don't feel like it, and you can choose to do the opposite of what you feel like doing. You can take control of your life,[14] or you can drift along waiting until something or somebody gives you a little motivation.

You can choose to live in accordance with the double-win philosophy, or you can let yourself get caught in the competitive "I win, you lose" way of living.

To a remarkable degree you can choose how you feel, how you react to stress, and how you handle frustration.

You and I can also choose how we manage life. We can choose how to handle the issues discussed in this book: stress, feelings, attitudes, relationships, marriage, family, career, decisions, money, our bodies, ourselves, and the spiritual parts of life. This is a book about choices. It assumes that people who manage their lives well are people who make wise choices.

Taking Risks

Making choices is risky. There is always the possibility that you will make the wrong choice. What if your choices arouse insecurities, create embarrassment, or reveal things about yourself that you don't want to face?

Long ago I discovered that people who refuse to take risks almost never grow. When we struggle with choices and risk making mistakes, we become better and more mature people. When we drift through life, avoiding change and sidestepping difficult decisions, life becomes dull and empty. We can try to avoid making choices by doing nothing, but even that is a decision. By doing nothing, we have passively chosen not to act. That isn't a very effective way to manage our lives.

I have a friend who is a business consultant. His work takes him into corporate boardrooms and offices of powerful business executives.

"They hire me to consult about their businesses," my friend told me recently, "but so often their own lives are in shambles." He continued:

> These are men and women who handle huge company budgets and answer questions at stockholders' meetings, but they can't keep track of their personal expenses.
> These are people who run giant corporations but can't run their families or control their teenagers.
> These are business leaders who remain cool, calm, and alert during lengthy labor negotiations but scream at their wives and never listen to their kids.

These are individuals who manage their careers and their companies with precision, but often these same people have broken down in the privacy of their massive offices and cried because they couldn't manage their own lives.

The shelves of local bookstores overflow with volumes on career development and business management. Almost every week I get at least one notice about some management seminar.

But the books and seminars rarely talk about self-management. They say little about getting your life out of neutral. Before we can really handle our work and our careers, we must learn to manage ourselves and take charge of our lives—like Ricky Hosea did when he prepared to walk through that hospital door.

Life management is risky and sometimes difficult. It's also possible. That's what we'll see in the pages that follow.

Levenson Locus of Control Scale

For each of the following questions, indicate the extent to which you agree or disagree. If you agree completely circle +3. If you disagree completely circle −3. There are no right or wrong answers. Directions for scoring will be given after you complete the test.

+3 +2 +1 −1 −2 −3   A.   Whether or not I get to be a leader depends mostly on my ability.

+3 +2 +1 −1 −2 −3   B.   To a great extent my life is controlled by accidental happenings.

+3 +2 +1 −1 −2 −3   C.   I feel that what happens in my life is mostly determined by powerful people.

+3 +2 +1 −1 −2 −3   D.   Whether or not I get into a car accident depends mostly on how good a driver I am.

+3 +2 +1 −1 −2 −3   E.   When I make plans, I am almost certain to make them work.

+3 +2 +1 −1 −2 −3   F.   Often there is no chance of protecting my personal interests from bad-luck happenings.

+3 +2 +1 −1 −2 −3   G.   When I get what I want, it's usually because I'm lucky.

+3 +2 +1 −1 −2 −3   H.   Although I might have good ability, I will not be given leadership responsibility without appealing to those in positions of power.

+3 +2 +1 −1 −2 −3 I. How many friends I have depends on how nice a person I am.

+3 +2 +1 −1 −2 −3 J. I have often found that what is going to happen will happen.

+3 +2 +1 −1 −2 −3 K. My life is chiefly controlled by powerful others.

+3 +2 +1 −1 −2 −3 L. Whether or not I get into a car accident is mostly a matter of luck.

+3 +2 +1 −1 −2 −3 M. People like myself have very little chance of protecting our personal interests when they conflict with those of strong pressure groups.

+3 +2 +1 −1 −2 −3 N. It is not always wise for me to plan too far ahead because many things turn out to be a matter of good or bad fortune.

+3 +2 +1 −1 −2 −3 O. Getting what I want requires pleasing those people above me.

+3 +2 +1 −1 −2 −3 P. Whether or not I get to be a leader depends on whether I'm lucky enough to be in the right place at the right time.

+3 +2 +1 −1 −2 −3 Q. If important people were to decide they didn't like me, I probably wouldn't make many friends.

+3 +2 +1 −1 −2 −3 R. I can pretty much determine what will happen in my life.

+3 +2 +1 −1 −2 −3 S. I am usually able to protect my personal interests.

+3 +2 +1 −1 −2 −3   T.   Whether or not I get into a car accident depends mostly on the other driver.

+3 +2 +1 −1 −2 −3   U.   When I get what I want, it's usually because I work hard for it.

+3 +2 +1 −1 −2 −3   V.   In order to have my plans work, I make sure they fit in with the desires of people who have power over me.

+3 +2 +1 −1 −2 −3   W.   My life is determined by my own actions.

+3 +2 +1 −1 −2 −3   X.   It's chiefly a matter of fate whether or not I have a few friends or many friends.

Scoring Procedures

There are three separate scales used to measure one's locus of control: the internal scale, the powerful others scale, and the chance scale. There are eight items on each of these scales. To score each scale add up your answers to the items for that scale. (These items are listed below.) To each sum, add +24. (This removes the possibility of negative scores.) The possible range of scores on each scale is from 0 to 48. A person could score high or low on all three scales. The higher the score on a scale, the more inclined the individual is to believe in that particular form of control.

Scale	Items	Your Score
Internal Scale	(A, D, E, I, S, R, U, W)	_____
Powerful Others Scale	(C, H, K, M, O, Q, T, V)	_____
Chance Scale	(B, F, G, J, L, N, P, X)	_____

Source: Hanna Levenson, "Activism and Powerful Others: Distinctions Within the Concept of Internal-External Control," *Journal of Personality Assessment.* 38 (1974): 381, 382. Used by permission.

Two

Managing
Your
Stress

Bernie closed his business today.

There were no customers left at closing time and only a couple of longtime employees stayed to the end.

Bernie flipped off the lights, locked the door to his once-thriving clothing store, nodded a silent good-bye to his co-workers, and walked alone to the darkened parking lot.

This is not the story of an elderly man retiring after decades of service to his customers. Bernie is only thirty-seven. He was scarcely out of college when he opened his store and began the policy of treating his customers like important people. He quickly established a reputation for being fair and honest, for selling quality clothing, for showing a healthy sense of humor, and for knowing the people who came into his store. He never forgot my name—or the names of the people in my family; he knew my shirt size

33

and remembered, better than I did, what hung in my ward-
robe.

But Bernie couldn't compete with the massive clothes
markets that have sprung up throughout the suburbs. The
sales people there seem to care more about their hourly
wage than about customers. The racks are stuffed with suits
and jackets of infinitely more variety than Bernie could have
fit into his little store. The prices are lower than the prices at
Bernie's, and the big markets stay open almost round-the-
clock.

Bernie's clothing business fell victim to a changing economy, but the man feels defeated, frustrated, and a failure.
His customers have wished him well and expressed appreciation for his services, but the darkened store stands, in
Bernie's mind, as a monument to his inability to run a successful customer-centered business.

Stress and Pressure

How do people like Bernie—or you and me—handle
stress, rise above life's temporary setbacks, and move
ahead? In finding an answer, it helps to distinguish between
pressure and stress. Pressure comes from the hassles and
challenges of everyday living. It may involve struggling to
handle kids who are demanding or uncontrollable, working
within time constraints that are unreasonable, competing in
a difficult business climate, trying to do a job when there is
high ambiguity and not much tolerance for mistakes, living
with deteriorating health or poor family relationships, striving to get along with difficult people, or trying to rise above
what have been called the three horsemen of failure: fear,
frustration, and fatigue.[1]

Pressure isn't necessarily bad, unless it is too intense.
Pressure can challenge, motivate, and inspire people to keep
moving. A ten-year study by University of Chicago psy-

chologist Salvatore Maddi found that many business executives welcome pressure. It adds interest and excitement to their jobs, allows them to be creative, and prevents boredom. When pressure builds, these people rarely get depressed and they aren't inclined to have ulcers or heart attacks. They are people with high resilience and the ability to learn from their pressure-filled experiences. Most of us aren't like that, but even we nonexecutives need a little pressure to keep life interesting. In our society people who live without much pressure tend to be static, uninteresting, and dull.

In this age of rapid change and future shock, most of us don't have to worry about lives that have too little pressure. On the contrary, our pressures more often become so intense that they cease to be stimulating. Nobody is challenged or much motivated by pressures that adversely affect our bodies, interfere with work effectiveness, undercut the stability of our families, or drag us down emotionally. Intense pressure causes breakdown and failures.

Stress might be defined as pressure that we no longer can handle. Stress begins when we lack the strength, skills, or self-confidence to cope with pressure. Stress wears down the body and undermines psychological stability. All of us need at least a little pressure to have fulfilling and interesting lives, but we don't need stress.

Executive Stress

The LaCosta Life-style and Longevity Center in southern California exists to help executives handle pressure and reduce stress. Most of the nation's chief executive officers have power, wealth, respect, and success, says the center director, but many live "in quiet desperation." The same individual who is on top of everything at work may have a personal life that is a "pile of debris"—an emotional wreckage.

Work stress has been divided into three types.[2] First is that which affects people who are perfect for their jobs, until the job changes. A worker may function efficiently until automation begins to take over. A highly skilled nurse may do well until she is confronted with new procedures that make her experience outdated. An executive may handle the business well until interest rates jump, foreign competition enters the market, or demand for a product changes.

This is what happened to my friend Bernie. He ran a successful men's clothing store until new competition put him out of business and temporarily eroded his self-esteem.

A second type of work stress comes to those who are in the wrong jobs. This includes people who are promoted into jobs too advanced for their talents. Unwilling to admit their inadequacies, they hang on until they no longer can cope.

Third, are those who are competent to do their jobs but who are thrown by some other event. Divorce, the death of a spouse, or the discovery of serious illness, for example, are impossible to ignore. Work efficiency suffers as a result.

When confronted with these stresses, many people refuse to admit defeat. They pay no attention to the warning signs, keep pushing, and eventually collapse physically, psychologically, economically, or in their family relationships.

Such collapse can be prevented when we make the effort to understand and apply the following principles of stress management.

Stress Can Be Self-Created

Barneveld is a quiet Wisconsin town with less than six hundred residents. Few had heard of it until the June night when a devastating black funnel cloud cut through the village, killed nine people, and blew away most of the trees and buildings. Pictures of the destruction flashed across television screens the next morning, and help began pouring in from all over the world.

The residents of Barneveld, Holland, after which the Wisconsin town had been named, held a plant sale and sent eight thousand dollars, plus a supply of tulip bulbs.

Six-year-old Nathan Renkes and his friend Jeff Zey held a read-a-thon in Green Bay and raised six dollars.

The *Wisconsin State Journal* in Madison started a fund that brought in more than a quarter of a million dollars.

But the nation was most impressed with the people of Barneveld. Adversity pulled them together and almost everyone pitched in to rebuild the town. Some picked up the pieces with apparent ease and went on with life. But there were others who began to buckle under a load of fear, grief, insecurity, and anxiety.

The Barneveld tragedy illustrated again that we each respond to stress in different ways. All of the residents experienced the same tornado at the same time. More than half of the homes and most of the businesses were demolished or damaged beyond repair. Everybody grieved, but some people recovered quickly while others didn't. The same external pressure that motivated some, immobilized others.

Findings like this have led some experts to conclude that stress is individualized and largely self-induced. Environmental events may put us under pressure, but how we react depends on ourselves. When we understand this, we are able to manage life more effectively.

S-T-R-E-S-S

When pressures get intense, it may help to think of a six-point formula built around the letters in the word *stress*.

S—*Situations* or stimuli in the environment start the stress process. In Barneveld it was a tornado. For Bernie it was business competition and realization that his store couldn't survive. For others it may be an inner fear or growing insecurity.

T—Triggers are body reactions touched off by the stressful situation perhaps even before we realize that is happening.

R—Responses within the individual can be of different kinds. Everybody knows that frightened rabbits freeze, fight, or flee when they are startled. People tend to do the same. Our bodies react automatically to the increased pressure. Often the heart beats faster, the adrenaline flows, the muscles get tense, and, physiologically, we are ready for action.

E—Evaluations follow. How we think about the pressure determines whether it will get worse, better, or stay about the same.[3] Some people expect the worst, see the despair, and wait for misery or failure to come out of every pressure situation. Others have a brighter outlook, try to keep things in perspective, see reason for being thankful.

Hans Selye, the world-famous stress researcher, concluded that two attitudes, more than any other, influence the quality of everyday life and the ability of individuals to handle pressure. Upon these two emotions, he wrote, "depend our peace of mind, our feelings of security or insecurity, of fulfillment or frustration, in short, the extent to which we can make a success of life."[4]

The most destructive emotion is *revenge*. It only serves to generate more revenge and self-destruction. In Selye's opinion, getting even has no virtue whatever. One of the biblical writers reached a similar conclusion centuries ago. "Watch out that no bitterness takes root among you, for as it springs up it causes deep trouble, hurting many . . ." (Hebrews 12:15 TLB).

In contrast "among all the emotions, there is one which,

more than any other, accounts for the absence or presence of stress in human relations: that is the feeling of *gratitude*."[5] Researcher Selye agreed with the biblical writers who long ago concluded that thanksgiving is a healthy response even in the midst of intense pressure.

S—*Seeing life differently* is one way of responding to pressure situations. At the LaCosta center they don't ask people to quit their jobs, slow down, or make radical changes in the way they live. "What we teach," says the director, "is a principle abhorred in modern society—moderation." People are encouraged to take an honest look at their lives and to ponder ways in which they might make changes.

Stress can be a warning sign that something has to give. If we don't change voluntarily, our bodies, minds, businesses, or marriages break instead and we are forced to make changes in the way we think and live. Otherwise stress becomes a killer—literally.

Clearly, it is better to take a look at our lives and move toward moderation now, before a breakdown demands immediate change whether or not we are ready.

S—*Step out*, then, to change your circumstances, your thinking, and your attitudes whenever pressures begin to build. It is possible to react to stress by moping or doing nothing. That isn't good life management.

Much more effective is a determination to keep things in perspective and to keep going as best you can despite the circumstances.

Two Elderly Ladies

I saw these principles illustrated in two aged women whose health and mental alertness began to fail as they reached the end of their lives.

Mrs. Finlay (that's her real name) was a remarkable lady

whose sense of humor and bright spirit shone through to the end of her life. When illness and arthritis slowed her down, she maintained a grateful attitude, found solace in her deep religious faith, and did whatever she could to help and cheer others in the nursing home.

Mrs. K., in contrast, complained bitterly, whined perpetually about her condition, and talked only about her problems and how things were never going to get better. She was the only person who wondered why nobody came to visit. Her griping made life miserable for herself and everyone else.

These two women experienced similar stresses. One chose to rise above the situation without denying its reality. The other created more stress by her own choices and mental attitudes.

The Effects of Stress Can Be Powerful

Meyer Friedman was on the move, even when he was growing up in Kansas City. He was still in grade school when he made the decision to later attend Yale and Johns Hopkins Medical School. His determined progress through the educational system resembled that of a high-powered Sherman tank. Soon he was established as a respected medical researcher and cardiologist who hardly slowed even when he began having symptoms of angina at age forty-five. A heart attack and coronary-bypass surgery came a few years later.

Dr. Friedman knows a lot about Type A behavior, the hostile, driven, high-pressured, impatient style of living that makes people more prone to have heart attacks. With his colleague, Ray Rosenman, Friedman proposed the term *Type A* in a book that appeared in 1974.[6] Sometimes called "the hurry sickness," Type A describes people who always push themselves, never have enough time, and rarely relax. They show four major symptoms, says Dr. Friedman: aggravation, irritability, anger, and impatience.

It was not until 1981 that the National Heart, Lung, and Blood Institute added Type A behavior to the official list of major coronary risk factors. For too many years, Friedman believes, doctors had been listening to their stethoscopes and not looking into the anxious faces of their self-driven patients.

Four Villains

Pressure and stress are too complicated to fit into neat categories. Management consultant Karl Albrecht suggests, however, that most of us struggle with stress that comes from four major sources.[7]

Time stress is especially common in America where we are pressured by deadlines, driven by a sense of urgency, and obsessed with ideas about "saving time," not wasting or "losing time," "making up for lost time," and "being on time." We have more clocks in this country than anyplace else in the world and many of us live with the feeling that time is "too short" or "running out." When we don't worry about time ourselves, others remind us of its importance.

Anticipatory stress, commonly known as worry, is a feeling of anxiety about some coming event. Sometimes we have reason to be worried, but often a sense of dread and fear comes in response to our own imaginations. We anticipate pressures and failures that never come. There are times when we get so distracted with worry that we actually "blow it" and bring about the very events we fear. Excessive concern about a potential problem can cause it to occur.[8]

Situational stress comes when we feel threatened and faced with challenges that seem at least partially beyond our control. These are times when we feel insignificant, incompetent, and unable to live up to our own or someone else's expectations.

Encounter stress is a tension that comes because of the actions, presence, or absence of people. When others act to put down, criticize, hinder, or undercut our actions, we feel under stress. Similar feelings come when we are surrounded by more people than we want to handle, or when we are lonely and lacking human contact.

Some of us are "people persons" who enjoy human contact and are highly gregarious. Others are more introverted and prefer periods of solitude. If you get into a job where you have greater or less human contact than you want, pressures and stress can build quickly.

Four Victims

Suppose you find that pressure is building and the stresses are increasing. How are you likely to react? There are four places where you can fall victim to stress.

The first of these is the *physical* area. Ulcers, headaches, back pains, heart problems—almost every disease and physical symptom can be created or made worse by stress.

Stress tends to weaken the body's immune system—that incredibly complex barricade that keeps out disease. When the anti-disease barriers come down, the potential for illness goes up. This is another way of saying stress can make you sick.

Stress can also affect us *psychologically.* Memory, efficiency, clear thinking, and problem-solving ability all decline when people are under stress. In his stress-management seminars, Dr. Friedman tries hard to convince high-powered career builders that their work would be more effective and their thinking clearer, if they could calm down and be less frazzled.

Stress also has a *social* or interpersonal effect. People

under too much pressure rarely show understanding or patience, build long-lasting intimate relationships, or get along smoothly with others. One seminar on life management lets hard-driving men listen to tape recordings of women whose husbands have recently died from cardiac failure. Many of the listeners wince as they hear descriptions of deceased men who sound like themselves. Often the descriptions portray men who were too busy to build warm, caring relationships with their mates and families.

Stress-controlled people also have difficulties building relationships with God. Their *spiritual* lives are often sacrificed on the altar of professional advancement and business success. People like this fail to realize that attention to religious values can help them relax. In turn, they are better able to handle the pressures of life.

You Can Manage Stress by Making Physical Changes

Somebody once suggested that there are over ten thousand counseling techniques in use today. I wonder if anyone has counted the stress-management techniques that come from seminar leaders and book authors? There must be at least several hundred, most of which are basic common sense. Almost none of these is new; they have been around for a long time.

Why, then, do so many of us ignore the familiar self-management principles and opt instead for continued stress and the painful effects that this brings?

Simple procrastination may be one answer. We're all busy with other things. Probably you agree that more exercise, less drinking, more rest, and a better diet would make you healthier, but you haven't quite taken the effort to start making these changes. If you're reading this book you should be congratulated for your willingness to consider better life management.

Congratulations!

Reading is a step in the right direction, but it is easy to put a book aside and do nothing to change ourselves in ways that will shift our lives out of neutral. Most of us prefer to put off till tomorrow what we can't or won't find time to do today.

Maybe you've also convinced yourself that the stress which hurts others surely wouldn't harm you. This is a common way of thinking. It's the idea that "others have to worry about these things, but not me. I can handle stress fine."

I thought of this recently when I was one of the first to arrive on the scene of a serious motorcycle accident. Two young people were lying still on the pavement and bleeding profusely. Before climbing aboard the bike, neither had bothered to put on a helmet. Perhaps they had thought that others might need helmets, but not them.

In this highly technical society it is easy to assume that psychology, wonder drugs, or medical science can always fix us up if we do begin to fall apart. Sometimes that happens. More often, however, stress-related problems arise unexpectedly and affect health in ways we didn't anticipate and sometimes can't fix.

John D. Adams is a California business consultant who specializes in stress management. He suggests another reason why most of us do nothing to reduce our pressures. When we encounter books like this one or read articles on stress management, writes Adams, it is easy to be overwhelmed by all the suggestions telling us how to change. Some people throw up their hands in frustration, decide they can't put all the recommendations into effect, and end up doing nothing. Others rush to make wholesale changes in their life-styles. They try to change everything at once, and when this is combined with an already overloaded schedule, failure is almost inevitable.[9] Is it any wonder that busy people easily give up?

The questionnaire at the end of this chapter might help you think about your own stresses and ponder how these can be handled.

Shape Up

Nobody is surprised anymore to read that the body and the mind work together. When we take care of ourselves physically, we think more clearly and better handle life's increasing pressures.

You may want to consult a physician before making major changes in your physical routines. Until then, remind yourself of some basic facts.

1. *Physical activity* helps reduce tension, anger, depression, and intellectual sluggishness. Walking, jogging, swimming, or sports can be relaxing, unless you create more stress by competing on the playing field the same way you compete in the office.

Even without an intensive exercise program, you can get into the habit of climbing stairs instead of taking the elevator, walking across the parking lot instead of driving for ten minutes looking for a space near the door, and taking a short brief walk after you have been sitting for a while.

2. *Diet control* helps reduce stress. Avoid too much sugar, coffee, alcohol, salt, and snack foods. Be careful about self-medication. Even over-the-counter drugs can be habit-forming and harmful.

Several years ago, my wife took off forty-five pounds through a Diet Center program. Later she went to work as a diet counselor and, at my request, helped me reduce my bulging middle. I learned to eat a more balanced diet. I was reminded that extra weight takes a long time to build and doesn't come off permanently through fast crash diets. I discovered that weight loss is easier when another person gives help or encouragement. I learned all the excuses for going off the diet "just this once," and I became aware that nibbling is a common but self-defeating way of responding to pressure.

3. *Rest* helps us cope with stress. College students sometimes stay up all night writing papers but even resilient young bodies can't go on without sleep forever. Burning the candle at both ends eventually leads to burnout and physical collapse. If we don't rest our bodies, eventually they get the rest they need by breaking down and forcing us to stop.

You Can Manage Stress by Making Mental Changes

I once was approached by a film producer who wanted to make a series of movies on stress management. After some hesitation I agreed to the project and entered enthusiastically into working on scripts and making movies in living color.

Today I look on this as an unsuccessful venture that for me was a good learning experience. I feel positive about what I said in those movies, but the producers promised more than they could deliver. When the films appeared, the color quality was clearly substandard, the technical production was amateurish, the financial backers didn't get their profits, I never got paid, and the man who did most of the filming suddenly died from what appeared to be a stress-induced heart attack.

Strange and sad, isn't it, that we can think almost constantly about stress management but still do nothing about changing our own stressful life-styles?

This does not have to happen. You can manage many of your pressures and reduce stress by using some common, proven mental stress-reduction techniques.

Talk to Yourself

Do you ever talk to yourself? Probably all of us do but some of the things we say are inaccurate and self-defeating.

I once was invited to speak at a major conference held annually on the West Coast. The man who met me at the airport spoke in glowing terms about the past speakers. He told me of their brilliance, insights, humor, and captivating speaking styles. He was trying to be positive by including me in this select group of powerful communicators. The more he spoke, however, the more inadequate I felt. Later, alone in my hotel room, I concluded that it would be impossible to live up to such expectations. Soon I had convinced myself that I was going to fail, that the audience would fall asleep shortly after the speech began, and that my lecture would probably ruin the whole conference.

Before I gave the address next morning, I had to change my thinking. By more positive self-talk I convinced myself that I probably wouldn't fail and that nobody's conference or career would collapse if I did. This self-talk restored my confidence and my presentation was well received.

Whenever you feel depressed, frustrated, hounded by hassles, or pushed by pressures, ask yourself if you are mentally feeding yourself a line that is distorted and simply untrue.

Visualization

Some emotionally distraught or immature people live in worlds of fantasy, worlds filled with imagination and hopes for things that will never come to pass. Such distorted thinking is unrealistic and of little value in handling stress. But imagination can still be helpful.

Next time you feel a stress buildup, close your eyes for a few minutes, breathe deeply, and imagine yourself in a quiet, relaxed place. This simple exercise can slow down your heartbeat, untense the muscles, and make you calmer as you return to handle your problems. Music can have a similar effect. It can relax the body so you are better able to cope.

Some people use mental images to plan and rehearse future meetings, performances, or job interviews. Wishing, of course, doesn't make it so, but mental rehearsing can help you cope with problems privately before you have to handle them in reality. You can also think about your fears or past failures and try, mentally, to forgive yourself or to see the past in a more balanced perspective.

While you're thinking, don't forget the immense value of prayer, tears, and reading—including the perusal of an occasional distracting novel.

Tackling the Pressures Head-On

Ultimately, of course, problems have to be faced and solved directly. You have to ask what really causes the pressures, what you can do about them, and what you may have to live with and accept.

If you are like most people, eventually you will come to recognize that none of us can handle all of our problems alone. It may be "the American way" to be independent and individualistic, but sharing your struggles with others who care is a better way. It helps you get a clearer perspective on situations and gives input from other people as you ponder and take action to change.

You Can Manage Stress by Making Life-Style Changes

A lifetime of research has led Meyer Friedman to conclude that Type A behavior can be changed. He changed himself and demonstrated, through a major government-sponsored study, that people can slow down, learn to relax, greatly reduce the risk of heart attack, and still succeed in their careers.[10]

With increasing frequency, it seems, physicians and medical researchers are telling us that the best route to good health and reduced stress is through changes in life-style. One study of seven thousand adults surveyed their conformity to seven old-fashioned health habits: no smoking, moderate or no drinking, seven or eight hours of sleep per night, regular meals with no snacks in between, breakfast every day, normal weight, and regular moderate exercise. The health of people with all seven of these habits was better than the health of those with six. Those with six of these habits were healthier than the people who showed five, and so on down the line. When forty-five-year-old men were compared, the average life expectancy was 21.6 more years for those with zero to three good health habits, and 33.1 years remaining for those with six or seven.[11]

Maybe you would prefer to work yourself to death. Many people do, and some companies expect employees to be workaholics. Is this really what you want out of life? Is this really what you choose for yourself and your family? Is it worth pushing to reach the top if you lose your family, your health, and your joy of living in the process?

These are questions that each of us must answer individually. How you respond to questions like these largely influences how you handle stress and how you manage your life.

I suspect my friend Bernie, that former store owner, is grappling with some of these questions. "I know the clothing business well," he told me before closing day. "I haven't given up. I can build a career on my strengths and live successfully with a lot less pressure than we've had during the past couple of years."

I doubt that Bernie reads much poetry. Busy people sel-
dom do. Still, he might find it interesting to ponder four
lines from an eighteenth-century poet named William
Cowper.

> *A life all turbulence and noise may seem*
> *To him that leads it wise and to be praised,*
> *But wisdom is a pearl with most success*
> *Sought in still waters.*

The Task, Book 3

Sometimes we need to pull away from the turbulence and
noise of life, and retreat—mentally or by ourselves for a few
minutes or longer—into a place of quiet and stillness. If we
don't take the time to ponder our life-styles and control our
pressures, these will take control of us.

That isn't good life management.

If you didn't do so earlier, perhaps now is a good time to
fill out the questionnaire at the end of this chapter.

Stress and Change Questionnaire

Part 1

Please fill in the blanks below to indicate changes that are taking place in your life. BE SPECIFIC, but try to be brief. If you need more space, use extra paper. For the present, please ignore the boxes at the right.

1. How are you changing in terms of:
   Your physical appearance_____ ☐
   Your physical abilities_____ ☐
   Your energy level_____ ☐
   Your sexual behavior_____ ☐
   Your work capabilities_____ ☐
   Other?_____ ☐
2. Within the past three years, what changes have you seen in the following? (Ignore areas that do not apply.)
   Your marriage_____

   _____ ☐

   Your sexual life_____

   _____ ☐

   Your relationship with your parents_____

   _____ ☐

   Your relationship with your children_____

   _____ ☐

   Your relationship with your superiors at work_____

   _____ ☐

   Your relationship with fellow workers_____

   _____ ☐

   Other relationships_____

   _____ ☐

3. Now consider your work and career.
   What is getting better?_____

   _____ ☐

What is getting worse?_____

_____ □

What is most satisfying about your work?_____

_____ □

What is least satisfying about your work?_____

_____ □

4. Think now about the neighborhood or society in which
   you live.
   What is good about it?_____

   _____ □

   What is bad about it?_____

   _____ □

   What affects you most?_____

   _____ □

   What makes you optimistic about the future?_____

   _____ □

Part 2

Now go back over the list. In the boxes at the right put
  2 next to the items that you find *very stressful*
  1 next to the items that you find *somewhat stressful*
  0 next to the items that you find *not stressful*

Part 3

1. Please look over the list again. For each item that you
   marked 1 or 2, write below what you have done to reduce the stress. You may need more paper to do this. For
   the present, ignore the lines on the right.

   _____ ____

   _____ ____

   _____ ____

   _____ ____

   _____ ____

   _____ ____

_____ _____
_____ _____
_____ _____
_____ _____

2. Now look at the above. In the spaces at the right write:
   H next to the things that **H**elped a lot
   HL next to the things that **H**elped a **L**ittle
   DH next to the things that **D**idn't **H**elp
   MW next to the things that **M**ade matters **W**orse

3. Based on your reading of the chapter, what are specific things you can do to reduce stress in the future? Write your conclusions in the space below.

_____
_____
_____
_____
_____
_____
_____
_____

4. Think of a person or persons who could help you with your stresses. Write their name(s) below. Will you ask for their assistance?

_____
_____
_____

5. In the space below, write one specific step you will take to reduce your stress within the next week.

_____
_____

6. Mark your calendar to go over this questionnaire again one month from today.

Three

Managing Your Emotions

I t was an outrageously self-righteous sermon.

The young priest later admitted this himself. His harangue about not caring for the less fortunate had fallen on deaf ears. The congregation of Manhattan College students was unimpressed and unmoved. Only one of the worshipers bothered to give a response, and it wasn't very affirming.

"What about you, Father?" a student asked, perhaps with a touch of cynicism. "Why don't you practice what you preach?"

Within months the priest was doing just that. He apologized for his smugness, left the college, and moved into a tenement apartment on New York's Lower East Side. His goal was to be a chaplain to the large drug-addict population, but for months he was snubbed by suspicious neighbors (some of whom thought he might be a narcotics agent),

robbed repeatedly, and flooded with feelings of discouragement, loneliness, and compassion for his hurting neighborhood.

One cold midwinter night, two girls and four boys aged
fourteen to seventeen knocked at his door and pleaded for
shelter. Father Bruce Ritter didn't know this at the time, but
those six kids were to be the first of thousands. For almost
two decades they have been coming—runaway teenagers,
alcoholics, drug addicts, and prostitutes—many bearing the
scars of rape, frequent beatings, torture, and disease that
oozes from the cesspool of Time Square's sordid, anything-
goes, sex industry.

Father Ritter received national exposure when *Reader's
Digest* published the story of his difficult and compassionate
outreach to the exploited youngsters of New York.[1] He has
appeared on television talk shows, spoken at hundreds of
meetings, and heard the acclaim of those who might describe him as a North American version of Mother Teresa.

But the bills still keep piling up, the local exploiters keep
creating resistence, and the needy kids keep coming. Sev-
enty percent don't stay. Unschooled, unskilled, and lacking
in self-confidence, many return to the drugs, alcohol, sex,
and violence of the streets. There they market the only com-
modity that is theirs to sell—their own bodies. Many destroy themselves in the process.

Common Feelings

How do you feel when you read about people like Father
Ritter? In the comfort of a secure suburban home, it is easy
for me to admire the priest's dedication, feel a tinge of guilt
because I lack his commitment, and think about sending a
donation to his work.[2] If I am honest, I admit feelings of
sadness over the way those street kids are treated. I feel
angry over their exploitation but have trouble getting really

incensed about a world that is so far removed from my own. I feel gratitude that somebody is doing something to reach these young people, and I admire the volunteers who respond to Father Ritter's job description for those who might choose to help.

"Come work with me," he says. "Give me a year of your life and I'll give you a chance to feed the hungry, clothe the naked, tend the sick. I'll provide room and board and pay you $10 a week. Plan on three hours of prayer daily, and that's not negotiable. You'll need the strength you get from it to remain effective in the work you'll be doing."[3]

In contrast to the workers who respond to such a summons, you and I are more likely to be concerned about our families, anxious about our careers, or worried about paying the bills. Maybe you are enthused about your work and hobbies, excited—or depressed—about the progress of some local sports team, or happy as you think about a coming vacation.

All of these are common feelings. If you let your eye skim back over the previous several paragraphs you will notice that a number of feelings have been mentioned. Guilt, sadness, anger, gratitude, concern, anxiety, worry, enthusiasm, excitement, depression, happiness—these are feelings that add zest and variety to life. Without them we would exist in lackluster states of barren boredom.

For most of us, that isn't a problem. Instead of too few emotions, we more often are controlled by a variety of feelings that we sometimes aren't sure how to manage.

Emotions Are Okay

It may seem strange and unnecessary to begin our discussion of feeling-management with a statement in defense of emotions. But there are people in our culture who still think that big boys don't cry, good Christians never feel sad or angry, strong people don't get depressed, or that macho men shouldn't weaken themselves by experiencing or showing feelings.

Emotions Are Universal

Let us begin, therefore, with the reminder that everybody has emotions; they are part of being human.

Psychologist Archibald Hart has argued that there are two extremes of emotional experience, either of which can be harmful.[4] People who deny their emotions and pretend they don't exist are people who avoid life. In contrast, those who feel too much emotion or let feelings take control, are people whose attitudes can destroy life. For all of us there has to be a healthy balance between these two alternatives. This balance is found when we learn to manage our emotions.

The influence of emotions was discussed recently in a management seminar attended by a group of senior military officers. During their careers, these men had seen hundreds of scared recruits, angry drill sergeants, lonely GIs, and unhappy families. As we talked about ways to help others manage feelings, the seminar participants began to open up about their own insecurities, worries, guilt, and discouragements.

Each of these people was in the midst of a successful career. Each was enthusiastic about life in the military, but they all knew that work is not done efficiently, interpersonal relationships do not go smoothly, and countries are not defended securely when the people in uniform are worried, unhappy, discouraged, or otherwise distracted by feelings. This is rarely mentioned in basic training, but sometimes feelings are harder to handle than guns or military discipline.

Emotions Can Be Useful

Sometimes life management is difficult because we try to deny our feelings and pretend they don't exist. We fail to notice how emotions can add excitement and diversity to life, and we forget that feelings often can be useful warning signs.

Emotional pain, like physical pain, lets us know that something is wrong and needs to be corrected. To ignore these warnings can be as harmful to health as the decision to overlook the physical symptoms that tell us something is wrong with the body.

> ## Emotions Are Tied to Thoughts and Actions

Have you ever pondered why sophisticated grown men sometimes dress in outlandish hats or act in almost bizarre ways when they are caught in the excitement of a championship sports event or American political convention? For a while, they allow emotions to take over while they respond in ways that are not completely rational.

Something similar happens when there are race riots, outbursts of political violence, or attempts at suicide. Temporarily, emotions are allowed to overpower clear thinking and to guide behavior.

To manage emotions we must recognize that feelings, thoughts, and actions are all interrelated. Change one of these and the other two will be affected.

For example, suppose you *feel* emotionally depressed. This will affect the way you *think* and the way you *act*. If you are angry or worried, these feelings will keep you from thinking about other things and will interfere with the efficiency of your actions at work. More positive emotions can have the same effect. The young man in love has difficulty concentrating and thinking about his job or avoiding mistakes at work. Emotions can influence every area of life.

The influences also work in reverse. If you act in a way that is foolish or embarrassing, this affects how you feel and how you think. If you think in some distorted way—as I did before my lecture on the West Coast—this influences how you feel and how you act. Feelings, thinking, and actions always are related.

This is worth remembering when you consider self-management and ways to get your life out of neutral. Since feelings are tied to thoughts and actions, one way to change feelings is to change how you think or how you act.

Have you ever noticed how hard it is to turn off a feeling willfully? You can tell yourself to stop worrying but that rarely changes anything. The worry still persists. Tell a friend there is no need to feel guilty or no reason to be depressed and anxious, but the feelings will still be there. Emotions don't usually respond to intellectual instructions. We can't turn off feelings like we shut off a tap.

We must view emotions and feelings as signals telling us to *think* differently or to change the way we *act*. Since thinking, behaving, and feeling all go together, we can change one of these by altering the others. Feelings may be hard to change, but we can think differently or behave in a different way. To manage emotions, therefore, work on changing your thoughts and actions.

Suppose you feel anxiety about a coming job interview. The anxiety may indicate that you need to prepare more carefully, that you are overexaggerating the importance of the interview, or that your insecurity and poor self-concept are getting in the way. It won't do much good to tell yourself to stop being anxious, but it could help to think differently about yourself and the interview (perhaps using self-talk), to prepare more carefully, or to ponder ways that would help you relax physically before your interview time arrives.

Feelings and Voters

Politicians like to talk about issues, give speeches about injustice, and make promises about their future actions, if elected. Go to a campaign meeting and you might think that elections are fought, won, and lost on the basis of rational thinking alone.

Social scientists know differently. Studies at several American universities show that feelings influence voters more than party identification or discussion of a platform. Regardless of where they stand on issues, the candidates most likely to win are those who stimulate hope, arouse pride, and keep people from being afraid or angry. It also helps if they do something that looks like a show of strength or decisiveness. This lets voters think the candidate has leadership abilities, even when the decisive actions are not very wise. In addition, good looks, facial expressions, style of delivery, and gestures can influence voters in ways that experts still don't understand.[5] The candidate who assumes that clear thinking and concise speeches are more important than image and emotion is a candidate who probably will lose.

In politics, as in every other area of life, thinking, behavior, and feelings go together.

Emotions Should Be Acknowledged and Expressed

When I was in college, my psychology professor sometimes compared emotions to bananas. Fruit that begins to ripen, he said, can't be ignored. You can hide browning bananas by putting them on a cupboard shelf behind the cans, but their smell and influence will soon make their presence known.

At times, all of us treat feelings like rotting bananas. We may try to push fears, discouragements, grief, lusts, or loneliness out of awareness, but that doesn't snuff out their impact. Feelings that aren't admitted and expressed can drag us down psychologically and harm us physically.

Robin Graham was a young man who had a dream and a desire for adventure. At age sixteen, accompanied by two small kittens, he sailed his twenty-four-foot sloop, *Dove*, out of the harbor of San Pedro, California. Five years and thirty thousand miles later he accomplished his goal of sailing around the world *alone*.

The Graham adventure story was illustrated in *National Geographic*, told in books, and made into a popular movie.[6] People admired the young man's courage and determination. Some were critical of his parents but others applauded their willingness to encourage and let their adventurous son fulfill his dream.

I was impressed with Robin Graham's openness about his feelings. "Loneliness," he wrote, "was to grip me for a thousand days and nights. At times it was almost as if loneliness had climbed aboard *Dove* with cold, clammy hands that reached out for my throat and heart—and stomach. Loneliness was to be an enemy that I never quite managed to conquer. The enemy knew my weakest moments. It knew exactly when to strike."[7] It led to tears, sadness, and sometimes self-pity.

Graham faced the "most miserable moment" of his journey when one of the cats died. He cried as he buried the animal under a palm tree, and for two days he stayed in *Dove's* cabin, grieving, crying, and feeling sorry for himself.

That was not unhealthy. Here was a young man who admitted his feelings, faced them squarely, and didn't try to deny their existence. Perhaps this is one reason he kept his sanity during those long days of sailing without human companionship.

Inappropriate Ventilation

During the turbulent sixties, some radical therapists encouraged people to express their feelings wherever and however they wanted. This is irresponsible and immature ventilation. For a while it may feel good to spill out feelings, but it does little to help us manage life effectively.

Uncontrolled emotional expression can hurt others and infringe on their rights, but it also harms you. People who are cynical, for example, have a much higher risk of heart disease than those who are less cynical.[8] Individuals who freely express anger and frustration don't get rid of these feelings. Instead, the more you spew out anger, the madder you get.

What, then, is a better way to express feelings?

Healthy Expression of Feelings

First, admit to yourself how you feel. Robin Graham had nobody to tell but himself, but he still found value in honestly admitting his loneliness and grief. We can't manage emotions if we pretend they don't exist.

Sometimes this self-admission isn't as easy as it sounds. Have you ever felt a vague sense of emotional discomfort but been unable to pinpoint what was wrong? I sense this at times when I feel "down" but can't decide why. After a period of hours or days the reasons may pop into mind with greater clarity, but occasionally we have to live with that inner tension without much awareness of what is happening.

It is then that sharing your feelings with others can be

especially helpful. This is the second guideline for healthy emotional expression. Another person may see things about your life or feelings that you can't see yourself.

Expressing feelings to others can backfire if you aren't careful. Things said in honesty, with a sincere desire for openness and free interaction, can sometimes hurt very deeply or lead others to be defensive and angry. How, then, do we more appropriately express feelings to others?

• Use "I-statements." To say, "I feel upset and angry about this situation," somehow seems less volatile than, "You make me mad!" I-statements are less likely to arouse defenses or ignite arguments because they aren't intended to blame others. It is difficult to argue with someone who is stating how he or she feels.

• Describe your feelings. Instead of pretending that things are fine when they are not, be honest in admitting, "I feel put-down," "I feel guilty," "I feel sad," or, "I feel angry." At times you may want to use analogies: "I feel like garbage," "I feel like I'm talking to a brick wall," "I feel like I'm invisible."

• Express your feelings nonverbally as well as in words. Robin Graham found that crying was an appropriate and therapeutic way to express feelings—even for men. Laughing relieves tension at times, and everybody knows the value of hugging or shouting. Jogging or other physical exercise creates chemical changes within the body that help to reduce depression.

In expressing feelings, be careful to consider where and when. Shouting is appropriate at football games but not in most church services. Swinging a golf club when you are frustrated can be helpful and therapeutic; throwing a chair at your wife is not. The old idea of counting to ten before you respond is good psychology. The ten-second delay lets you gain enough composure to keep you from doing something foolish and self-defeating.

Emotions Can Be Controlled

New Year's resolutions usually get broken. Everybody knows that, but two researchers at the University of Missouri wanted to know why.[9]

The investigators knew they couldn't get answers by studying people whose goals were general or vague. If you decide some year to "become a better person," or to "be happier," for example, there is no real way to know later whether this has happened or not. You may think there has been change, but your goals are vague and it would be difficult for anyone to study them scientifically or precisely.

Suppose, however, that someone has a specific goal—to stop smoking, for example, or to lose thirty-five pounds, increase his number of dates each month, or raise his college grade-point average. These can be measured, and it is possible to carefully observe how people manage to bring about these changes in their own lives.

This was the goal of those midwestern researchers. Their study found that the best self-managers

    —use a variety of techniques; if one doesn't work, they try something else;

    —are persistent and willing to work at a goal longer than people who fail to change;

    —monitor their behavior, often using charts of progress or other records that let them keep a self-monitoring eye on their actions;

    —reward themselves whenever they succeed; self-reward is important for successful self-management; and

    —keep flexible and aware of individual differences; they realize that the same diet, study routine, or problem-solving approach doesn't work for all people or all problems.

These findings are important for all of life management. They are especially helpful for people who want to control habits, but they also apply when we are trying to control emotions.

Control Your Emotions by Your Thinking

Feelings, thinking, and actions, as we have seen, are closely related. To control our feelings and emotions, it often can be helpful to change our thinking.

If you heard a hundred words of praise today and one criticism, what would you remember? For almost all of us the answer is the same. One little criticism, even from an unreliable source, can drag you down and make you feel discouraged, self-condemning, and sometimes embarrassed.

When this happens, you can choose to stay down or you can change your thinking and largely pull yourself up from life's temporary discouragements. Feelings frequently are determined, and often changed by, choice. We can control how we feel by our thinking; we are not passive victims.

John Ehrlichman is a remarkable example of this principle. From his position of prominence and power in the Nixon White House, Ehrlichman became one of the most despised and ridiculed casualties of Watergate. He served time in a federal prison in Arizona, saw his marriage collapse, and was ostracized by many of his countrymen.

"Why didn't you commit suicide?" a magazine editor once asked. Mr. Ehrlichman admitted that he had considered the idea, but chose to take another course of action.

"I had to decide for myself whether to live or to die. That was the choice," he told the questioner. *"No one else could pull me out of my self-pity.* If I couldn't live with the truth that many people will never accept me as a person, if I have to depend on others for my self-esteem, then I must choose death. If I wanted to live, *I had to quit my depression.* I had to say my life had value, and I had to mean it. I chose life."[10]

What about you, or me? When we are criticized, do we wallow in self-pity and discouragement?

Too often for me the answer is yes. It takes time and practice to challenge my own thinking and choose to see things differently. I am learning, however, that critics aren't always right. Sometimes criticisms come from people who have limited information, biased perspectives, or such hostile personalities that they never see good in anything. Often the criticisms say as much or more about the critic as they do about the one who is criticized.

My reaction to the criticism may also say something about me. It can trigger feelings of personal inadequacy and make me feel like a failure. Even when the criticism is rare or inaccurate, I sometimes feel like quitting or condemning the critic. Words of criticism often hurt because they remind me of weaknesses that I suspect might be true.

What do we do if criticism is valid? Can we learn from the critic and go on? Do I have to assume that I'm no good, a failure, and completely incompetent because someone has criticized me? Do I stop myself cold, immobilized because I've made an error or have failed at some task?

Thoughts like these help us avoid unpleasant feelings and let us choose to control our emotions. There are times, of course, when the feelings arise from physiological reactions that can't always be controlled mentally. Even then, however, there is evidence that humor, positive attitudes, and balanced thinking can affect one's physiology and indirectly change emotions.[11]

Control Your Emotions by Your Actions

Within hours of his departure on that trip around the world, Robin Graham discovered a therapeutic technique that did wonders to pull him out of depression and feelings of loneliness. He got busy. Sometimes he felt too sad to get moving, but the need to alter course or cope with some weather change or other emergency would jolt him from his lethargy. Once he got active, he felt better.

How often have you seen this in grief-stricken people? The ones who keep active make a better recovery. Runners know that jogging relieves tension and can alter one's outlook on life. Insightful married couples often learn that the best way to rekindle a fading love is to do loving acts for each other. People who know what is causing their feelings can often take practical action to change the situation that produces the tension. In all of these examples, changed feelings follow overt actions.

Many years ago, psychologists assumed that hitting a punching bag or throwing a tantrum could be another action-oriented way to get anger or other feelings "out of your system." This view is no longer widely accepted. Research has shown that aggressive behavior can *create* more anger, instead of dissolving it.[12]

More effective is a form of self-control that admits the feeling, engages in tension-reducing physical activity, tries to see the cause of anger in a different light, and takes whatever action is necessary to change the cause of the anger. By combining actions with thinking, the anger is better controlled.

Control Your Emotions by Sharing

Probably you know people who love talking about their troubles, anger, depression, worries, or feelings of inferiority. A few even like to talk perpetually about their joys and feelings of enthusiasm. This talk bores all who are forced to listen and does nothing to change the feelings of those who use so many words to rehearse their emotions.

From this it should not be assumed that talk is always bad. On the contrary, it is healthy to share your feelings with a friend or counselor. By facing and dealing with emotional issues in this way, you get a clearer perspective on how to change your thinking and actions. People who talk perpetually about their feelings often have no real desire to change and fail to learn from the responses of others. But for those who sincerely want to share and seek solutions, talking can be very therapeutic.

Many people find this same therapy in prayer. For some, prayer is a form of self-talk that helps the pray-er think more clearly. If you believe, as I do, that God exists as a compassionate Being who cares for individuals, who hears our prayers, and who answers, this can be one of the most powerful ways of controlling emotion and managing your life more effectively.

Harmful Emotions Can Be Overcome

Many years ago, I gave a series of talks that later found their way into a book. The publisher titled it *Overcoming Anxiety* and to my surprise it was sold to more people than any of the books I have written before or since.[13]

Do you want to overcome anxiety, depression, guilt, or other troublesome feelings? The place to start, once again, is with your mind.

Emotional Causes

By now you know that emotions are complex. There is rarely a single source of anxiety, worry, anger, self-hate, or any other feeling.

Depression, for example, may have a number of causes. Sometimes endocrine changes, fatigue, illness, or other physical influences make us depressed. Depression also

comes when we feel helpless or trapped in unpleasant jobs
and other situations that we can't control. Some psychologists think depression comes most often when we feel inadequate, failing, or lacking in self-esteem. Others know that
depression often comes from anger; when anger festers
within, it frequently drags us down. In almost all of these
cases, depressed people feel some kind of a loss—of a loved
one, of a close relationship, of a dream, of a valued pos-
session, of anything else that is important.

Like all other feelings, depression will not be managed
and overcome until you uncover its causes. If the feeling is
of recent origin or not intense, you probably can figure out
the cause yourself. If not, talk it over with a friend or
trained counselor.

In looking for causes, try to avoid those common reason-
ing errors that might lead your thinking astray.[14] For example, when two events occur, one right after the other, it does
not follow that the first causes the second. When two events
occur at the same time, it does not follow that one is related
to the other. Popular old wives' tales about emotion also
tend to be wrong. Just because somebody says so, it doesn't
follow that "depression always comes from sin," "grief just
means that people are feeling sorry for themselves," "getting even is the best way to deal with anger," or "keeping a
stiff upper lip will cure self-pity and depression."

Watch for this kind of careless thinking in all of your life
management. Thinking errors aren't limited to your efforts
to control emotion.

Emotional Chaining

Have you noticed how emotions go together? Sometimes
one can lead to another, making you feel worse and worse.
Suppose you lose a job and feel discouraged. This may lead
to anger and the decision to write a nasty letter to your for-

mer employer. Then you might feel guilty for reacting so quickly, self-pity because you are out of work, depressed because you don't have a job, annoyed with yourself when you snap at someone who offers help, and embarrassed when you apply for unemployment compensation.

This has been called "emotional chaining."[15] It is a common tendency to create new emotions out of those that exist already. It is a challenge in life management to sort out these feelings, to deal with them one at a time, and to move back to deal with the original emotion that started the whole process in the first place.

Emotional Coping

If you live in the north, you may have noticed that people tend to get depressed during long winters. The January cold, the dreariness of February, and the biting winds of March leave us feeling lethargic and discouraged.

It came as no surprise to northerners when researchers discovered that part of the problem is a lack of light. Winter blues, it was found, tend to lift when people are exposed to greater periods of real or artificial sunlight.

When we change the amount of light that comes into a room, we are changing the environment. We can do something similar with music, the color of walls, furnishings in a room, noise reduction, or the elimination of crowding. For lonely people, the presence of a pet can help change feelings. For senior citizens, a couple of plants to care for can work therapeutic wonders.

All of this suggests that moods are easily influenced—by the environment, by what we eat, by the people with whom we live or work, by the amount of sleep we get, by exercise. These influences help us relax so we can think more clearly about the causes of our emotions and take action to bring change.

I don't know how Father Ritter handles his feelings. He
must get frustrated and discouraged. Maybe, at times, he
thinks of the doctorate he got many years ago in medieval
theology and wonders if he should leave the continuing tragedies of Times Square and return to academia. I have
heard he gets angry with politicians, welfare agencies, pros-
ecutors, and the courts for their failure to deal with the sexual exploitation that he sees every day. But I suspect he also
feels a sense of satisfaction to be doing something for those
who otherwise are without hope.

I once received a book from a stranger who had titled his
work *Emotions: Sometimes I have them/Sometimes they have me.*[16]
That's an accurate description for most of us. The goal of
emotional management is to control feelings, before the
feelings control me.

The questionnaire that follows might be a useful guide to
help you with some of that emotional control.

Thinking About Feelings

1. Please read the following list of emotions. In column A
   write:

   O if you feel this *often*
   S if you feel this *sometimes*
   R if you feel this *rarely*
   N if you feel this *never*

A		B	C
_____	angry	_____	_____
_____	anxious	_____	_____
_____	appreciated	_____	_____
_____	bitter	_____	_____
_____	caring	_____	_____
_____	confused	_____	_____
_____	criticized	_____	_____
_____	depressed	_____	_____
_____	disappointed	_____	_____
_____	embarrassed	_____	_____
_____	enthusiastic	_____	_____
_____	fearful	_____	_____

Now continue as above for the following emotions. There
are several blank lines at the bottom for other emotions that
you might want to add.

frustrated	guilty	happy
hating	helpless	impatient
inadequate	jealous	joyful
lonely	loved	loving
peaceful	put-down	respected
sad	thankful	threatened
unwanted	wanted	_____
_____	_____	_____

2. Read over the list again. In column B write how you would like to feel. Use the same symbols (*O, S, R, N*).

3. Now go over the list one more time. In column C put a check where there is a difference between columns A and B.

4. What could you do so there is less difference between columns A and B? Try to be specific. Write your conclusions below or on a separate paper.

5. Think of some recent situation that made you feel really _____. (Fill in the blank with *angry, sad, excited,* or some other emotion.)

6. How did you manage your emotion?

7. How could it have been managed better?

8. As a result of this experience, and your reading, what have you learned about managing emotions?

9. You may want to repeat 5–8 above using another example. It could also be helpful to share your conclusions with some other person.

Four

Managing

Your

Attitudes

K evin Robinson is a writer. Every day he sits at a small desk in the spare bedroom of his Kansas City home and pecks away, with one finger, on a trusted electric typewriter. Sometimes he writes articles, but Kevin Robinson's real love is the trilogy he started several years ago. Volume one is almost complete.

As a young man, Robinson worked at various jobs—farming, selling, pumping gas in a service station, driving a truck, working as a forest ranger. He has always loved sports and once worked at a ranch teaching troubled kids.

That was where his life changed—radically.

Standing on a dock one summer afternoon, he leaned against a railing that gave way and pitched him into the lake. Kevin Robinson broke his neck, and to this day he is paralyzed from the chest down. Typing, with the only finger strong enough for the task, was part of his physical therapy. For fun, he started a fantasy novel and soon was thinking about his trilogy. He writes from a wheelchair, his paralyzed arms resting on the desk, his one finger turning out a novel.

Life for this man has been filled with hardship. Failed business ventures, court fights with his medical insurance company, fire that destroyed all his family's belongings, a car accident that seriously injured his wife—these might have overwhelmed a lesser person.

But not Kevin Robinson.

"I tend to be overly optimistic until proven wrong," he told an interviewer from *Writer's Digest* magazine.[1] "If one door closes, I'll bang on the wall until I find another one."

This is a man who manages life by managing his attitudes.

What Are Attitudes?

All of us talk about attitudes, especially when we're describing somebody else. We accuse our kids of having bad attitudes, tell our work colleagues that they should change their attitudes, learn from motivational speakers that we all need positive mental attitudes, and see signs outside the cocktail lounge promising how alcohol will adjust our attitudes. Psychologists design tests to measure attitudes, and politicians worry about voter attitudes, but the rest of us rarely give our own attitudes a thought. We fail to realize the importance of attitudes in life management.

Simply defined, an attitude is a way of thinking about some group, person, event, or institution. We can have attitudes about racial groups, individuals, political movements, happenings in the neighborhood, the church, the government, and almost any other issue. Most attitudes are either positive or negative. Some are held firmly while others don't seem to be very important. A few attitudes, like love of country or belief in freedom, are shared by almost everybody. Other attitudes are private and may be held by nobody else.

All of us have attitudes about ourselves. What kind of a person am I? What are my strengths and weaknesses? What can I do well? What kind of a personality do I have? How do other people see me?

When I was a boy growing up in Canada, we had a neighbor lady who was active in the Salvation Army. Sometimes I would visit in her home and one day I asked Mrs. Ritchie to write in my new autograph book. In her careful, old-style penmanship she inscribed these words:

A boy is not what he thinks he is,
But what he THINKS, he *is*.

To my preteenage mind, this didn't make any sense at all but now, years later, it is the only thing I remember from that old autograph book. Opinions about ourselves may not mean much, but we really *are* what we think.

Attitudes—what we think about life, work, ourselves, and others—are important in any plan for life management.

Attitudes and Actions

Attitudes aren't something you can hold in your hand, like a book or a piece of fruit. They are hard to measure, even with psychological tests, and most of us can only guess about the attitudes of others by watching how people act or by listening to what they say. Kevin Robinson's friends think he has a positive, optimistic attitude toward life. They have reached their conclusions by listening to him talk and by watching his never-say-die persistence as he works on his novel, one letter at a time.

Sometimes we get confused because what people say isn't the same as what they do. "I'm not prejudiced," proclaims your neighbor who invites everyone to his backyard picnic except the Pakistani family who lives down the street. "I try to be a good Christian," says your hypocritical boss who never goes to church and is known for shady business dealings in the community. At times like these, actions speak a lot louder than words. Your real attitudes are more often revealed by what you do than by what you say.

Attitudes may be long-standing and well entrenched, but most of them can be changed. Talk to someone of a different race, religion, or ethnic background, and your previous attitudes are likely to be altered, especially if you are willing to face and shed personal biases. The attitudes you have toward family members, work associates, community leaders—even attitudes you have toward yourself—can be changed in ways that will improve your life and make it more easily managed.

Many of Life's Problems and Most Solutions Begin in the Mind

The distinguished United States senator from Mississippi gestured toward a small plaque in his office. It had only two words: LOOK AHEAD.

"This is part of my philosophy," stated John Stennis. In his mid-eighties, the oldest man in the Senate was talking about his career in politics.

"As a young lawyer I used to have to listen to people lamenting the past. You can't do that. You have to look ahead. I realize life's not altogether what you make it. But that's part of it. What you make yourself."

While men twenty years his junior were starting retirement, Senator Stennis was still looking ahead. He had survived a bout with cancer and a recent strenuous political campaign to hold his Senate seat, but the interview with a newspaper reporter looked to the future, not to the past.

"How would you like to be remembered?" the reporter asked.

"I haven't thought about that a whole lot," Stennis replied. "You couldn't give me a finer compliment than to say, 'He did his best.' I get satisfaction about doing the best I can."

People like Senator Stennis know that problems, frustrations, and difficulties often come from sources beyond our control. Several years ago, when robbers beat up the elderly senator, stole his wallet, and pumped two bullets into his stomach and thigh, he faced a life-threatening crisis that was not of his own choosing. But even then, he was looking ahead, determined to survive and intent on going back to work. Perhaps as much as anything else, this mental attitude took John Stennis to full recovery.

People like this use their minds to look ahead; others sit immobile while they lament and ponder the past.

Some use their minds to plan violence or wars; others think of practical ways to attain and keep peace.

Some let their minds dwell on things that are wrong with a spouse, a job, or a neighborhood; others see what is good and work to make things better.

Some think of their problems and develop a "poor-little-me-isn't-it-awful" attitude; others admit their difficulties, then think of ways to adapt and keep moving in spite of pain and obstacles.

You have heard it said, I suspect, that the mind is the biggest sex organ in the body. What the mind thinks about sex often is translated into action when the opportunity arises.

Can the mind also be the strongest source of violence, the greatest cause of interpersonal tension, the most powerful threat to a stable marriage, or the biggest reason for vocational failure? If so, there is hope. Change people's thinking, starting with our own minds, and we can move more freely toward peace, marital stability, career success, and effective life management.

Dale Galloway is an Oregon minister who rebuilt his life after a series of problems left him feeling hopeless and in despair. Reflecting on these experiences, Galloway concluded that your attitude can make you or break you; heal you or hurt you; give you friends or create enemies; make you uptight or put you at ease; make you miserable or give you happiness; lead you to failure or make you an achiever.[2]

Whenever I feel discouraged I'm not inclined to read the rah-rah positive mental attitude literature that has helped others in similar circumstances. For me, and maybe for you, it is more helpful to start with the simple realization that many of my problems are created or made worse by my own thinking.

My own thinking is the place to start finding life-management solutions.

Many of Life's Diseases and Much Healing Begin in the Mind

Have you ever noticed that widows and widowers often get sick and sometimes die shortly after the death of their mates? At one time we described these widow deaths as the result of a broken heart, but medical science has found a more scientific explanation.

Whenever we experience the intense stress of grief, the body's immune system—the part of our physiology that helps us fend off disease—temporarily becomes less effective. As a result, it is harder for the body to fight disease and viruses. Sickness and sometimes death come, therefore, because the mental stresses of losing a loved one have made the body less disease resistant.

Findings like this led one researcher to title his book *Mind as Healer, Mind as Slayer*.[3] The author cited reams of research to show how the mind can create, or make us more susceptible to, hypertension, arteriosclerosis, heart attacks, strokes, migraine headaches, arthritis, bronchitis, emphysema, and a variety of other diseases. Anger, discouragement, frustration, driving determination, time pressure, tension, anxiety—these can all influence the body and contribute to its breakdown. Many people are literally killing themselves by refusing to alter their attitudes or to change their life-style habits.

The Good News

Just as mental attitudes can bring disease and health problems, they can also stimulate healing and the prevention of serious illness. This is good news. Your mind can't keep you from ever getting sick, but it can do a lot to bring healing when you do get down physically.

Almost everybody has heard of Norman Cousins. His story has been repeated perhaps hundreds of times, but he still remains a great example of a man whose mental attitude contributed significantly to his healing—twice.

The first time came when Cousins learned he had a rare disease of the tissues that hold the bones together. The doctors gave him one chance in five hundred of recovering, but Cousins determined to do what he could to beat the odds. He knew that stress and anger can harm the body by altering its chemistry, but he wondered if faith, hope, love, humor, confidence, and a will to live could help heal the body by creating positive chemical changes.

With his doctors' consent, Cousins stopped medication, reaffirmed his will to live, and experimented with the restorative power of laughter. By watching humorous movies or listening to tapes of humor books, he discovered that "ten minutes of genuine belly laughter" could give him at least two hours of pain-free sleep. In his personal experiment, Norman Cousins demonstrated what has since been supported by careful medical research—positive attitudes facilitate healing. A very wise man said something similar many years ago: "A cheerful heart is good medicine" (Proverbs 17:22).[4]

When Cousins had a serious heart attack, he was able to test his theories a second time.[5] He concluded, as have numerous medical experts, that despair, panic, foreboding, fear, hopelessness, or depression can hinder healing and often make an illness worse. In contrast, attitudes of hope, love, confidence, and a will to live—all sprinkled with a sense of humor—can trigger healing secretions throughout the body and contribute significantly to the healing process.

This was the kind of attitude that speeded Ronald Reagan's recovery following the assassination attempt in the early weeks of his presidency. As the president was wheeled in to surgery, he looked at the doctors with a twinkle in his eye and declared, "I sure hope you guys are Republicans!"

Motivation and Persistence Depend on the Mind

Following a seminar on life management, a man raised a thought-provoking question. "I have trouble with a lack of motivation," he said. "I can recognize a problem but have a continual inability to start toward a solution. What I need to do is clear, but how to get going isn't."

Probably there are many reasons for lack of motivation, including the following:

• *Lack of energy.* It is hard to get going when we feel tired, drained by other responsibilities, or dragging because we haven't been getting enough sleep. Sometimes we feel too lazy to get moving, but even the weather can slow us down. Dull dreary days are depressing; long summer heat waves rob us of vitality and enthusiasm.

• *Fear of failure.* It is easy to make plans but then do nothing to put our plans into action. There may be a good reason for this inactivity. Once you take action and start moving you face the possibility of failure. What will you do if somebody misunderstands or criticizes? When you don't want to risk failing, you are reluctant to move.

• *Setbacks.* Suppose you get started and then encounter a setback? In the title of one of his books, Robert Schuller proclaimed: "When the going gets tough, the tough get going." That's inspiring and motivating. But for most of us a paraphrase of this slogan is more accurate: "When the going gets tough, it's tough to get going."[6] Obstacles, frustrations, and other difficulties can be depressing and immobilizing.

• *People.* Don't always blame yourself for a lack of motivation. Sometimes other people can block your progress, convince you that success is impossible, and keep you from getting started. These challenges from others are difficult to resist at times.

I wonder how many people at some time plan to go on a diet but never get started because of these obstacles? Sometimes these would-be dieters lack the energy, are bothered by the prospects of failure, worry about jokes that could come from nonsympathetic friends, keep encountering setbacks such as business luncheons and tempting desserts, or lack encouragement from others. Diet counselors report that many women have difficulty sticking with diets because their husbands, who often want slimmer wives, nevertheless refuse to be supportive when their spouses try to maintain a rigid eating schedule.

So How Do We Get Going?

A lack of motivation must be attacked in the mind. Start by determining what you want to accomplish. Be specific.

Then, make some plans. How will you reach your goals? What step-by-step procedures will you follow? What is the first thing to do? What is the second step?

Set a time limit, at least for the earlier stages. Try to be realistic. Don't be so easy on yourself that you aren't motivated to get moving, or so unrealistic that you are certain to fail.

Think of some self-rewards. When you complete each step, how will you reward yourself?

Think about the obstacles that might get in the way. Awareness of these can be a good step in overcoming them.

Keep a record of your progress. This can be motivating, especially if you have charts or other visual reminders of how you are getting along.

While I was writing the above paragraphs, an author friend called and mentioned, in passing, that he was having motivational problems as he worked on a book. He deals with this in ways that apply some of the above principles. They are principles that I too have found helpful.

Before starting this book, for example, I did a great deal of reading, outlined the chapters, and presented the material in several life-management seminars. Maybe I spent too much time on these activities because I realized, one day, that the publisher's deadline was approaching fast and there was limited time to get my thoughts on paper. This should have been motivating but it threatened to immobilize me instead.

So I made a schedule, decided how many pages I could realistically write in one day, blocked out the hours for writing, cleared my calendar of distracting influences, and started on page 1. I have a little chart on which I check off my daily progress. A recent heat wave and visits from out-of-town guests threatened to slow my progress, but I'm still on schedule. I reward myself by doing something diversionary after each chapter is completed, and we are planning an overdue family vacation as soon as I get to the end. If these words get into print and you are reading them in a book, then you know that my self-motivation program worked.

Peak Performers

Charles Garfield was a young computer programmer when he landed his first job. His employer, the Grumman Aerospace Corporation of Long Island, had an exciting challenge: to design and build the Lunar Excursion Module that would be the first manned craft to land on the moon as part of the Apollo 11 mission.

It didn't take long for the young programmer to get caught up in the excitement of this vision. Everybody in the company was motivated by a powerful commitment to an innovative and important mission. With increasing frequency, once-ordinary employees were turning into superachievers.

Charles Garfield wondered why.

After Neil Armstrong's historic walk on the moon in July of 1969, Garfield left the aerospace industry, went back to school, completed a Ph.D. program in clinical psychology, and has devoted himself ever since to a study of what he calls "peak performers."

Peak performers are people like you and me who face obstacles and sometimes don't feel very motivated, but who believe that they will "make it" eventually. Peak performers are people who have learned the art of self-management. They know that motivation is largely tied to thoughts and mental attitudes.

They also share similar characteristics. Garfield studied over five hundred peak performers, trying to discover what motivated them to persist and achieve. The research uncovered six common attitudes that almost all of them possess:

1. *A sense of mission.* People who become peak performers have a vision—some kind of a goal or ideal that is worth pursuing with all their energies and creativity. This is an internal decision to excel. According to Dr. Garfield, potential peak performers who don't have such a mission make it their mission to find a mission!

2. *A commitment to getting results* within a period of time. These people set goals and make practical plans to reach these goals. They believe that a well-defined goal-directed plan will give the enthusiasm and energy they need to keep going. They are action-oriented people who keep abreast of new information and keep plugging until they get things done.

3. *Self-management through self-mastery.* Peak performers take initiative, consistently evaluate themselves, know their strengths and weaknesses, trust their ability to do the job, and strive for self-mastery. They remember their missions, but also are aware of details. Often they engage in self-talk that lets them rehearse activities mentally before they act.

4. *Team building/team playing.* This is a variation of the double-win philosophy that we discussed in chapter 1. Peak performers delegate power and responsibility, stretch the abilities of others, urge people to take educated risks, strive for cooperation, encourage one another, try to avoid placing blame, and do what they can to stimulate a "we" mentality. Often they think of success as a group goal.

5. *Course correction.* Everybody makes mistakes, hits snags, and sometimes runs out of stamina. This does not knock out the peak performer. He or she learns from failure, tries to be flexible, is open to doing things in a different way, and keeps aware of stresses that might hinder efficiency. These people are committed to getting results and are willing to change course if necessary.

6. *Change management.* Unlike people who wait for change and then adapt, peak performers anticipate what is coming in the future and learn new skills to help them keep up. They are always learning, always considering alternatives, always updating the mission, and always expecting to succeed.[7]

This could be an overwhelming list, discouraging to ordinary people with ordinary jobs. But Charles Garfield believes we all can be peak performers. The characteristics and attitudes of these unusual people are not inborn. They are learned and can come to anyone who takes the time to acquire and apply them.

The place to start with such attitude formation is in the mind. The questionnaire at the end of this chapter may help with your planning.

> ## Bitterness and Forgiveness Start and Stop in the Mind

Corrie ten Boom was a remarkable woman. Her deep Christian faith, her determination to aid persecuted Jews during the Nazi occupation of Holland, and her horrible incarceration in a wartime prison camp have all been recorded in a deeply moving film, *The Hiding Place.*

Following the war that brought death to most of her relatives, Miss ten Boom found herself face to face one day with a former Nazi. He was a man whom she recognized, a man who had been one of her tormentors in the prisoner-of-war camp where she had spent so many miserable months.

Corrie ten Boom had given a talk on forgiveness and the former gestapo agent had been in the audience. Now he was approaching her with hand outstretched. What should she do? Should she take his hand? Should she turn away from the one who had caused such misery and contributed to the death of her beloved sister?

The war-scarred Dutch lady hesitated, but only briefly. She extended her hand, spoke words of forgiveness, and felt a tremendous peace flood her whole being. Corrie ten Boom knew that revenge and bitterness destroy; forgiveness heals.

Frustration–Aggression

Every beginning psychology student learns that aggression is the most natural response to frustration. When we feel we've been treated unfairly, criticized unjustly, or stopped from reaching our goals, it is easy to react in anger.

Often that anger spills out in hostile words, cynical attitudes, or open violence. Sometimes it is held inside where it eats away at our attitudes, robs us of joy, drains us of physical vitality, and sometimes drags us down into depression. When anger is allowed to fester so it turns into a persisting bitterness, it can—as we saw in an earlier chapter—undermine emotional stability and take away any inner sense of well-being.

Go back into history and you can see a clear example of this in Israel's King Saul. Following a significant military battle, the army came home for a victory parade and the people turned out to applaud and cheer. "Saul has slain his thousands," they sang, but the king didn't care for the rest of the lyrics, "and David his tens of thousands."

Saul was angry and jealous. Threatened by this rival (who eventually ascended the throne), the king became bitter and obsessed with thoughts of murder. In time, the bitterness tore apart Saul's family, almost destroyed his nation, eroded his mental stability, and led to his death by suicide.

In this life, few things are more destructive than persisting attitudes of bitterness.

Frustration-Forgiveness

It is easy to be aggressive and bitter. It is much harder to forgive without holding grudges.

Forgiveness takes time. Emotional wounds sometimes go very deep and they rarely heal quickly. Even when we forgive, with sincerity, the memories of past hurt may pop back into mind when they are least expected. At such times, remind yourself that you have decided to forgive and that you plan to stick with your decision.

Forgiveness takes effort. Forgiveness is more a choice than a feeling. It often involves telling someone that you forgive. It involves telling yourself, sometimes repeatedly, that you forgive. It involves refusing to keep dwelling on past injustice. Instead, forgiveness is a willingness to give up your rights. It is a decision to not seek revenge or strive to get even.

Forgiveness is risky. Forgive someone and he or she may laugh, call you naive or a pushover, take advantage of you, or criticize. I know a man who deserted his wife and left the family in shambles. After a long struggle, the wife reached a point of being able to forgive, but her husband didn't take this seriously. He laughed when she talked about forgiveness. I also suspect she went home feeling at peace while he went away carrying his load of embarrassment and guilt.

Forgiveness is personal. It starts with you and it may involve forgiving yourself. Everybody makes mistakes. We all fail and at times do things that hurt others. Wallowing in guilt over the past will do nothing to help change our attitudes. Instead, we must learn—perhaps with the help of a counselor or friend—to admit failures, to forgive ourselves and others, then to go on with life.

Forgiveness involves a positive attitude. On a December Sunday morning several years ago, a young pastor entered the pulpit of his church, stood before his congregation, and proclaimed the joys of Christmas on the saddest day of his life. Hours before, a stranger had handed him the divorce papers and he had watched helplessly as his wife and two small children boarded an airplane and departed, never to return.

Could he forgive his wife for leaving? Could he forgive himself for failing as a husband and father? Would he slip into bitterness, self-pity, and negativism?

The answers didn't come immediately, but eventually he saw the importance of changed attitudes. He was able to forgive and go on with life when he learned to cultivate positive ways of thinking. What was his formula?[8]

1. Try to be an ambassador of good words; say something kind, encouraging, or positive to everyone you meet.

2. No matter what happens, look for good in the situation and you will find something that will give you reason to be thankful.

3. Let your mind dwell on what is positive—good, worthwhile, commendable—instead of thinking all the time about the negative and critical. When negative thoughts slip into your mind, try not to dwell on them. Avoid gripe sessions that can pull you down and make you bitter.

4. Don't let your mind dwell on thoughts or fantasies that are suggestive, lewd, vulgar, perverted, or immoral. You can't think about garbage and expect your mind to stay healthy, unpolluted, and sound.

5. Look for what is good in others. Try to point this out verbally by expressing appreciation and encouragement. If you look for good characteristics in others, and in yourself, you will find them.

6. Remember the power of prayer. Religions, especially the Judeo-Christian religions, are built on the idea of for-

giveness. Ask God to forgive you. Pray that you will have the strength, willpower, and ability to forgive yourself and others.

Character Building Begins in the Mind

Four well-known television comedians were recently observed having lunch in a New York restaurant. There was no banter coming from the table, no joking, and almost never a smile. These professional laugh-makers gave every evidence of being unhappy people when they weren't performing on the stage.

At times, all of us can put on a pretty good show. You can feel sad but look happy, be angry but turn on the charm, feel incompetent but impress others with your capabilities. Like professional performers who cover up their real personalities, you and I can keep others from getting behind the masks that we present to the world.

But what are you *really* like? Do you know?

If somebody wrote an accurate character description of you, what would it say? Could you write a description of yourself?

More important, what would you like it to say?

Some psychiatrists believe personality is molded by the time we are five or six. But characteristics surely are not like cement that hardens early, can't be changed, and is broken only with difficulty and destruction.

We are, instead, more like plants that are able to grow, change, and blossom. Some people don't grow much. They let their bodies get out of shape, their minds get dull, and their creativity and enthusiasm wither. People like that probably aren't reading this book.

Others, like you, want to keep growing and blossoming. These are people who can be peak performers. They are always learning, always looking for the bright things in life, and always thinking of ways to improve their lives and build better character traits. Maybe that is one reason why they read books on life management.

Change is never easy, but change is possible. Think of the kind of person you would like to be. You can be more friendly, sensitive, compassionate, encouraging, positive, or self-confident. Character changes take root slowly, but the seed of change is planted in the mind.

Tucked under the calendar on the desk where I work is a list of traits that I would like to see in myself. I look at this list frequently, ask God to make me a man who has these traits, and look for every opportunity to act as if these traits were part of my personality. As I grow older, they are becoming more and more a part of me.

Character development is an important part of life management. It begins with our attitudes.

Planning Ahead

1. What is your purpose in life? It may take a while to think about this, and your purpose may change as you go through life, but try to answer this question now.

   _____

   _____

2. What will be the date ten years from today? _____
   What would you like your life to be like in ten years? List at least three goals that you would like to have accomplished by then.

   A. _____

   _____

   B. _____

   _____

   C. _____

   _____

3. Please look at goal A. How could you reach that goal? List some specific steps (practical things you must do) to get to your goal. (You may need more than five steps.)

   A. _____

   _____

   B. _____

   _____

   C. _____

   _____

   D. _____

   _____

   E. _____

   _____

4. How will you reward yourself when you complete each of these steps? _____

_____

5. What obstacles might prevent you from reaching your goal? If you list them, perhaps you can better avoid them.

_____

6. How will you measure progress toward each goal? Is there something specific that will indicate that you have really passed each step? _____

_____

7. Please repeat steps 3–6 using another item from the list under question 2.

8. Many people find it helpful to work with a one-year plan, a five-year plan, and a ten-year plan. Keep the plans flexible, however, so you can adapt to changing circumstances. You may want to revise your plans at least once a year.

Five

Managing

Your

Relationships

They call it the smallest show on earth.
The last of its kind!
The only remaining dog and pony show!
Every summer it winds its way through the cornfields and narrow roads of mid-America. Day after day the little "big-top" of the Culpepper and Merriweather Great Combined Circus rises on the outskirts of another tiny backcountry hamlet. The ten nomadic troop members—six performers, one workhand, two strong teenagers, and one young boy—work together to set up the bleachers and get the show ready.

Most of them have multiple jobs. When she isn't performing, aerialist Lynn Metzger sells tickets and works as the circus cook. B. J. Herbert, the show's only clown, runs the souvenir stand and sometimes operates the tape recorder that provides lively, canned circus music to accom-

pany the acts. Curtis Cainan does daredevil tricks on a revolving ladder then reappears with his animal act. There are
no lions or elephants. In addition to several goats, the circus
has only a few performing dogs and half a dozen Shetland
ponies. That's why they call it a dog and pony show!

Years ago, there were dozens of one-ring shows like this,
crisscrossing the country and visiting villages throughout
rural America. Now this is the only one left. Every night
after the show, the circus people take down their tent and
bleachers, load everything into a battered truck with red
sides and gilded circus lettering, then prepare to move out
next morning to another town.[1]

It would be interesting to know how this tiny troupe gets
along. Money is scarce; sometimes they don't earn enough
to buy gas to reach the next town. Privacy is limited; the
people live in trailers and RVs, but they eat together and
have almost no time to be by themselves. Resentment, discouragement, and interpersonal tension must surface at
times. If so, they probably are dealt with quickly—otherwise the little company would disintegrate from within.

Interpersonal Relationships

Have you ever wondered why some people—like that circus group—work together in harmony, but others have
trouble getting along? Why is there tension between husbands and wives, brothers and sisters, parents and children?
Why do college roommates clash, church congregations
split, and even "best friends" show distrust and disagreement? Why do you have conflict with your boss or tension
with the people at work? Why are there so many divorce
cases in the courts, acts of violence in the streets, labor-
management disputes, racial pressures, and conflicts be-

tween nations? Is there something innate that prevents human beings from getting along with one another?[2]

These questions would be meaningless if people were robots, all cast from the same mold, all with similar attitudes, opinions, and beliefs. If we were created like precut pieces of a jigsaw puzzle, then we might be able to live together in peace, interlocked into a pattern of stability.

But we are neither robots nor parts of a puzzle. We are unique, changing individuals who differ from one another in our past experiences, aspirations, attitudes, abilities, values, and views about life.

We are also social creatures. People like you and me do not live alone on islands. We live in contact with one another. We know it is neither good, possible, nor pleasant for humans to exist in isolation.

That is what leads to our tensions. Because we live in close proximity and because each of us is uniquely different from all others, we frequently find ourselves in conflict.

These tensions have a way of snowballing. Family feuds, political arguments, and office squabbles, for example, often begin with relatively insignificant issues; but minor disagreements can be like the tiny sparks that ignite a mighty forest fire. Suspicion, distrust, criticism, jealousy, and tension build to the point where interpersonal harmony becomes almost impossible, even when both sides sincerely want peace.

In times like this it is easy to fight or to leave. Many marriages end like that. The husband and wife disagree, argue, and hurt each other until one or both give up and walk out. It is harder to stick with the turmoil, to search for solutions, and to work at resolving differences. It takes time to manage our interpersonal relationships, especially when there is tension. You can't really win at the life-management game, however, until you learn how to get along with other people.

Getting Along With People Isn't Easy

This obvious fact is frequently forgotten. According to one historian, eight thousand peace treaties were signed between 1500 B.C. and A.D. 1860.[3] Each was supposed to bring permanent peace, but each lasted an average of two years. Even with our sophisticated technology and grasp of social psychology, we moderns haven't shown much (if any) improvement in this dismal historical record. Interpersonal tension started at the dawn of history and it's been going on ever since.

The reasons for this may be as diverse and as complex as the people involved.

The Fear of Closeness

For some, tension comes because there is fear of closeness.

It is risky to get close to other people. What if someone gets near enough to see weaknesses that you would prefer to hide? If people really could know you, would they still like you? Would they respect you, accept you? Would it hurt your career, harm your marriage, or weaken your self-esteem if others really knew what you are like?

Hardly anybody thinks consciously about these questions, but an inner fear of intimacy can keep us away from closeness. For some people, staying at a distance, keeping aloof from others, or stirring up trouble may all seem safer and less threatening than closeness and good interpersonal relationships.

The Cost of Closeness

When she was a second or third grader, one of my children had a "best friend" whose family left the community and moved to another part of the country. We watched our daughter grieve and understood when she told us, one evening, that she didn't want another close friend. "It hurts too much when they leave," she told us through her tears.

In this mobile society, haven't we all experienced the pain of separation? Maybe you have concluded, at times, that it hurts less to have no close friends, than to have friends from whom you might have to separate.

It is costly to develop good relationships with our families, our neighbors, our co-workers—and sometimes with our distant in-laws. It takes time and energy to build close friendships. Other people have a way of disrupting our schedules, hindering our plans, interfering with our careers, or wanting attention at inconvenient times. And there is always the possibility that close relationships will be torn apart by unexpected or unwanted moves.

The Western world is filled with hard-driving, career-conscious men and women who are unwilling to give the time or to pay the emotional price of building closeness with others. As the careers of these people go up, stability in their homes often goes down. Soon they see the real costs of neglected relationships—emotional pain, separation, loneliness, and sometimes deep feelings of rejection or anger.

Lack of Interpersonal Skills

Some people really want to build good relationships. They long for closeness and aren't afraid to give as much time, energy, or money as might be needed.

But they lack social skills. They are insensitive to others, don't know how to act in social situations, and never seem to say the right thing. Some of these people may be social misfits who draw attention to themselves or alienate others by loud talk and inappropriate comments.

Social misfits are not the only people who feel socially

awkward. At times, most of us feel uncomfortable and self-conscious with strangers or unfamiliar social situations.

Tim Stafford is a journalist who went with his wife to start a magazine in Kenya. The Africans extended a warm welcome but the Staffords soon met barriers. There were different values, views of history, perceptions of wealth, and ideas about time. Culture shock hit with startling abruptness and soon gave way to cultural fatigue. How easy it was to befriend other Westerners and withdraw to settings that were familiar. How much harder it was to understand, know, and communicate with the people of Nairobi.

The Staffords learned about sensitivity, listening, the need to understand, the importance of humility, and the value of "talking gingerly." In writing about his four years in Africa, Stafford identified one "master ingredient" for getting along in unusual or difficult social situations: persistence. "Those who persist in trying to make friends will nearly always succeed," he wrote. "They will overcome their handicaps."[4] But it isn't always easy.

Getting Along With People Starts With You

Looking at crises can sometimes help us understand how interpersonal relationships could be improved.

Almost everybody has heard of Kitty Genovese, the lady who was murdered several years ago while thirty-eight of her neighbors watched from their apartment windows without moving to call the police. Less familiar is the story of Andrew Mormille, a seventeen-year-old who was stabbed in the stomach while riding the subway. Eleven riders watched the stabbing but none came to assist the dying boy, even after his attackers had fled and the train had left the station.

Less dramatic but equally shocking is the experience of Eleanor Bradley. While shopping on Fifth Avenue in New York, the lady tripped and broke her leg. Dazed and in shock, she called for help, but busy shoppers and business executives walked by for forty minutes before a taxi driver finally took her to a hospital.

Stories like these led two psychologists to investigate why people fail to help in a crisis.[5] Why, they wondered, do car accidents, drownings, attempted suicides, and other tragedies sometimes draw great numbers of onlookers who do almost nothing to help the victims?

Before they intervene, the psychologists discovered, people must answer three questions in their own minds:

1. *Is there a need?* Is it possible that many of the people who walked around Eleanor Bradley didn't even notice? We have learned to keep out of other people's business and we know it isn't polite to stare. So we go our own ways and fail to see potential crises or other problems within our own communities or families.

2. *Is this an emergency?* Sometimes we notice changes but do nothing because we fail to see any need to act. Many of the people who passed Eleanor Bradley assumed she was drunk, so they left her alone. Since nobody else was stopping, many of the busy passersby assumed there was no emergency so they kept walking as well.

3. *Am I responsible for taking action?* After Kitty Genovese's death, the neighbors were asked why they didn't call the police. Everybody had noticed the beating and heard the screams. All of the neighbors knew it was an emergency but nobody dialed the police because everybody assumed this already had been done by one of the other neighbors.

A lot of us don't like to get involved in interpersonal squabbles. We dislike conflict and tend to avoid confrontation. When interpersonal tensions begin to surface, maybe you prefer to ignore them, wait for somebody else to act, or hope the problems will go away by themselves. Sometimes they do; usually they don't.

Emerging interpersonal tensions only go away when we recognize them for what they are—potential trouble signs; emergencies that need attention.

Where Do Good Relationships Begin?

Do you remember the story of the good Samaritan? A man was robbed, beaten, and left on the road to die. Two people passed by and did nothing. Maybe they didn't notice the man, although that seems unlikely. Maybe they didn't see this as an emergency—also unlikely. It is more probable that the passers were in a hurry, busy with other things, unwilling to get involved, and content to leave the wounded man for some good Samaritan who might stop to take action.

Does this describe you at times? Crises sometimes attract our attention and force us to act. But in day-to-day living it is easy to get busy with careers or other interests and fail to notice when distance grows between you and your spouse, when your children stop communicating, or when co-workers are increasingly uncooperative. An important step in building interpersonal relationships is to keep aware of others and to notice when tensions begin to develop.

When we have trouble getting along with others, it is easy to assume that somebody else should or will take action. If everybody makes this assumption—like Kitty Genovese's neighbors—then nothing gets done and the problems get worse.

When interpersonal tensions arise, sometimes you are the only one who can or will do anything to manage or change the situation. The solution to interpersonal problems may start with you.

Reasons for Inactivity

Even when we know the importance of getting involved, this often is difficult. Without meaning to do so, we can create or complicate interpersonal problems. Have you noticed how easily any of us can become

- Deaf: refusing to listen;
- Rigid: refusing to change;
- Narrow-minded: refusing to honestly consider any point of view other than our own;
- Stubborn: refusing to forgive;
- Ostrichlike: refusing even to admit that a problem exists;
- Elephantlike: refusing to forget;
- Self-righteous: refusing to admit that we may be part of the problem; or
- Threatened: refusing to risk taking some action?

These are not meant to be accusing thoughts. Who among us hasn't fallen into most or all of these categories? It isn't easy to see ourselves clearly and most of us don't recognize how our own actions may be contributing to interpersonal problems. Sometimes it takes a courageous colleague, a perceptive friend, or a loving spouse to gently point out how you are making tensions worse. Be thankful for such insights, listen to them, and be prepared to change.

When interpersonal problems appear, the effective self-manager has the courage to face the issues squarely. You can do this by answering two questions:

1. To what extent am I a part of the problem?
2. What can I do, specifically, to make things better?

**Getting Along With People Requires
Respect and Understanding**

Periodically I am invited to speak at conferences overseas. I enjoy the travel, but often have wondered if talks by foreigners really are effective—especially when we have to use an interpreter.

When I asked about this, a friend from El Salvador was willing to give his opinion. "We aren't stupid," he began. "We listen to lots of speeches and sermons given by visitors. Even when they talk through interpreters we can tell almost immediately whether a speaker looks down on us or accepts us as equals. When speakers talk down to us, we know they don't respect us, so we don't pay much attention. When they show respect and acceptance, they can communicate effectively."

My friend added that many visitors from North America fail the test. They rarely take time to understand the culture where they speak, they radiate an "I'm better than you" attitude, and, my friend added as graciously as he could, such visitors should stay home.

Point of View

My friend didn't use the term, but wasn't he talking about prejudice? Whenever we make a prejudgment about some other group or person, we are showing a prejudice. Even if you try to keep such views private, they tend to slip out in your actions, joking, or speech. Assume that some individual or ethnic group is stupid, and sooner or later you will say something or act in a way that betrays your beliefs.

Prejudices are not limited to racial or religious issues. You can be prejudiced toward women, adolescents, supervisors, politicians, doctors, neighbors, or members of your own family.

I know a teenager, for example, who has never been able to get along with her mother. The mother has definite views about teenagers, and the daughter has equally strong ideas about parents. There is some validity to both viewpoints, but the two fail to understand each other and rarely communicate because their prejudices keep getting in the way.

Good interpersonal relations involve a willingness to see and understand the other person's point of view, even if you don't agree. Remember the old Indian proverb: Never judge a man until you have walked a mile in his moccasins. We don't manage interpersonal relationships well until we try to understand others and respect them as people, even when we don't accept their beliefs or viewpoints.

Leadership

This principle of understanding and respect came to prominence recently in a study of leadership. Good leaders must learn how to manage people well and Warren Bennis wondered how this was done. Past president of the University of Cincinnati, consultant to four United States presidents, and currently professor of management at the University of Southern California, Bennis conducted an in-depth study of ninety businessmen, public servants, and leaders in the arts and sports. Most of the people are well-known; all would be considered successful.

Why were these people good leaders? To some degree they all shared four characteristics:

1. **Vision.** This was the one trait that all leaders had in abundance. Each had clear goals; some well-defined intentions or projects they wanted to complete.

2. **Persistence.** Each of the leaders was willing to work in

diligent pursuit of the vision, even when he or she encountered resistance, obstacles, and setbacks.

3. **Respect.** The leaders all knew their strengths and nurtured them. Equally important, all leaders respected others and tried to bring out the best in people. There was a willingness to listen to subordinates, to understand the perspectives of others, to see latent talent, and to encourage its development.

4. **Communication.** The good leaders knew how to communicate. Many were capable speakers and writers, but of greatest importance was the ability to make ideas vivid, dramatic, and understandable to others.[6]

How does this apply to those of us who are not the top leaders of science, entertainment, and business? Most of us won't reach the level of the Bennis subjects, but we too can develop a vision, persist in working toward goals, develop respect and understanding for others, and learn to communicate effectively.

Before we look more closely at communication, two additional conclusions of the leadership study can be of interest. To his surprise, Dr. Bennis found that most of his successful leaders were still married to their first wives and were enthusiastic about marriage. Apparently they had applied the four leadership principles to their own families and had built good relationships as a result.

The leaders were also described as people who strive to do what is right. A good manager, says Warren Bennis, is somebody who does things right. A good leader does the right things. The difference is worth pondering.

Is there any reason why the successful self-manager couldn't do both: do things right and do the right things?

Getting Along With People Requires Effective Communication

Young boys are great card collectors. Everybody knows that, including people who sell products to young people.

The executives of a chewing gum company decided recently to make their packaging more appealing by including cards for kids to give to their friends and classmates. I never saw any of the cards, but I heard about one that caused a great uproar.

The gum company called it innocent "insult humor," but it was devastating to the insecure twelve-year-old who one day received the "Most Unpopular Student Award" card from his classmates. Newspaper columnist Bob Greene wrote about it in his syndicated column and received a flood of letters from sympathetic readers.[7] Most had experienced similar taunts early in childhood and still were bearing the scars. Almost all felt compassion for the twelve-year-old to whom so much had been communicated by the message on a two-by-three-inch piece of thin cardboard.

Communication is like that. A few words, a gesture, a joking comment—simple things like these can hurt and create misunderstanding that lasts for a lifetime. Every counselor knows that communication breakdown is devastating to a marriage, and healing is not likely to come until the lines of communication are open.

You will never manage your relationships until you manage the art of good communication. The questionnaire at the end of this chapter helps with communication skills, but it also is important to understand why communication breaks down and how it can be improved.

Look at figure 1 and think of this as a picture of two brains. Suppose the brain on the left gets an idea (that's la-

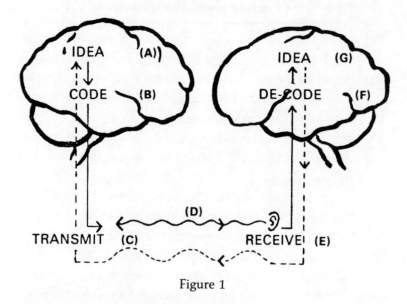

Figure 1

beled A) and wants to send it to the brain of the person on the right. To do this (notice the letters), the idea must

B—be put into some kind of a code, usually in the form of words or gestures;

C—be transmitted, by a note or verbally, using spoken words that come with gestures, tone of voice, and other nonverbal signals;

D—be passed from one person to another;

E—be received by the person who gets the message;

F—be decoded by the person on the right; and

G—be understood.

The person who gets the message doesn't just sit there like a zombie. He or she soon starts sending messages back (see the dotted line in the diagram) using all the same coding and decoding steps in reverse.

Communication failure can occur at any point in this little

chain. The sender can have a fuzzy idea (A), can express it in a confusing way (B), can mumble and not send it very clearly (C), can be talking in a noisy room so the idea can't get across (D), can be heard incorrectly (E), can be misperceived (F), or can be misunderstood (G). There are many opportunities for communication to break down. And the whole process gets complicated more if several people are trying to communicate at the same time.

But there is hope.

Effective Communication

We can learn to communicate more effectively, but it usually takes effort.

- *Think clearly.* Often we don't communicate because we don't know what we really want to say, or we don't think before we act. Those grade-school kids probably didn't realize how much the card would hurt their twelve-year-old classmate. Immature young people often are insensitive, but we who are older should be more careful about the things we communicate.
- *Express yourself carefully.* As clearly as possible, try to say what you mean to say.
- *Listen carefully.* This is the place where most communication breaks down. We don't listen to what the other person is trying to convey, or we fail to get the messages that come through gestures, facial expressions, tone of voice, or other nonverbal means. Before you reply, be sure you understand what the other person is trying to communicate.
- *Think before you respond.* How easy it is to jump to conclusions or to give quick answers that we might regret later.
- *Try to show respect.* Communication is better when we show the respect that was mentioned earlier. Sometimes this isn't easy, but try at least to see the other person as one who has a viewpoint that you need to understand—even though you might not agree.

• *Watch out for communication traps.* There are lots of these and we all get caught, especially if we are not careful.

Communication Traps

Communication is trapped by *double messages*. When a person says two things that contradict, we get a double message and aren't sure what to believe.

Double messages also appear when a person says one thing and does something different. Suppose the president of your company says employees are important but then he goes into his big office, closes the door, and has almost no contact with the workers. The president has sent a double message—and once again actions speak louder than words.

Do you send double messages to your spouse, your children, your colleagues at work, or others? If so, communication is likely to falter.

Communication is trapped by *loaded words*. "You never . . ." or "You always . . ." for example, often are followed by terms that provoke reaction and argument. Sarcastic remarks and "put-downs" are also loaded—and explosive.

Communication is trapped by *grievance collecting*. This is the tendency to keep a mental record of things that annoy you about some other person. All of this is stored in the mind like ammunition, ready to be pulled out and fired broadside during the next argument.

It is far better to deal with frustrations gently, one at a time, and when they first occur. When you have a disagreement, try to keep focused on the issue being discussed. Avoid bringing in past grievances. This only clouds the debate and incites anger.

Communication can also be trapped by *avoidance*. Watching television, talking about "safe" subjects such as the weather, failing to return phone calls, being too busy or excessively involved with work—these are all ways to avoid facing tense issues. The longer we put off the discussion, the harder it will be to communicate later, at a time when avoidance may no longer be possible.

Always remember that effective communication takes time, effort, and determination. If you want to manage your relationships effectively, you must be willing to work at communicating, even when you are tired, frustrated, and not inclined to be bothered talking.

Sometimes Getting Along With People Is Impossible

We didn't have time to find Stanley Street when our family visited Liverpool, but we heard about the simple statue that had been erected there, next to a building. Dedicated to "all the lonely people ..." everywhere, it is a life-size sculpture of Eleanor Rigby, the mythical creature created by the Beatles' song in 1966.

Hidden inside the bronze figure is a four-leaf clover for luck, a page from the Bible for spiritual help, a sonnet for lovers, an adventure book for excitement, and a pair of football socks for action. "I put them all inside the statue so she would be full of magical properties," said Tommy Steele, who donated the statue to Liverpool. But Eleanor Rigby looks sad, nondescript, and with no appearance of vitality.

Some relationships are like that. You may try hard to give them life or "magical properties." You may struggle to communicate, build rapport, and get along, but there still is conflict, distance, miscommunication, and coldness as vivid as the metal Eleanor Rigby statue on a biting winter day.

What do you do when you can't get along, regardless of how hard you try? The natural tendency is for people to avoid each other. Sometimes that helps, but it isn't always

possible or wise. Relationships, like problems, sometimes
get worse when they are avoided.

Nevertheless, there are ways to get your relationships out
of neutral.

• *Try to compromise.* On some issues you might never
agree with each other. Nevertheless, you can decide to live
with your two perspectives and still get along.

• *Avoid rehearsing your grievances.* When you keep dwelling on what is wrong with another person, *you* get angrier
and more frustrated. Try not to let your mind mull over and
dwell on the problems. Focus on things about the relationship that are positive and good.

• *Be skeptical of rumors.* One man says he believes none of
what he hears and only half of what he sees. That isn't a bad
philosophy.

• *Be careful of your imagination.* It is easy to make assumptions about what another person is thinking or doing, but
your assumptions may be wrong. Don't let your imagination control your thinking, especially when you have little
evidence to back up your speculations.

• *If possible, avoid the "hot" issues.* I have a friend with
whom I have a good relationship—until we start talking
politics. I have learned to steer clear of this issue whenever
we are together. Parents must learn to overlook some of the
annoying things about their children, so there can be a concentration on more important issues. Not every topic is
worth fighting for, or about.

• *Give yourself freedom to grieve when a relationship ends.*
Sometimes, despite your best efforts, there appears to be no
way to manage a relationship successfully. It is then that
you have to manage your feelings of failure, frustration, and
separation.

At such times there are stages through which people
often pass. The first is *denial,* when you refuse to believe
that the relationship has ended. Then comes *mourning.* This

isn't limited to grief over a death. People are sad and need a period of mourning when they divorce, move, lose a job, or in other ways are separated from close relationships. *Anger* often is part of the readjustment process, and then comes *adaptation* when emotions calm down, things get back into perspective, and life goes on more or less complete.

• *Avoid self-destructive tactics.* Once I was invited to speak as part of a conference on counseling. The day before my arrival, another speaker had strongly criticized me in public, and the audience was filled with people who expected me to swing back. I decided there would be no value in stooping to the same name-calling tactics as my critic. In my speech, I acknowledged our differences politely, then went on with my presentation. Some people might have been disappointed by the lack of fireworks, but in general the audience response was very positive.

Many of those people might have been familiar with the words of wise old King Solomon. They are words that summarize much of this chapter, words that are a good guideline for any person who wants to manage relationships successfully:

A gentle answer turns away wrath,
but a harsh word stirs up anger.

Proverbs 15:1

Getting Along With Others

This is not a test. Instead, it is a guide to help you think of ways to improve communication and better manage your relationships with others. Use additional paper if the space provided is not enough.

1. Think of some person with whom you would like to get along better. Write that person's name below:

   _____

2. What are some sources of conflict in your relationship? What are the issues that cause tension? List these below.

   _____
   _____
   _____
   _____

3. How do you cope with your differences? Do you argue, talk things over, avoid each other, fall into the communication traps that the chapter describes? In the space provided, jot down how you tend to deal with conflict.

   _____
   _____
   _____
   _____

4. Look back over the chapter, then list at least three specific things you could do to improve your relationship and get along better.

   A. _____
   _____

   B. _____
   _____

   C. _____
   _____

5. Which of these will you start working on first? _____

6. When will you start? _____

7. What will you do to improve your relationship during the next week? Be specific. _____

You may want to make a copy of these two pages and fill them in again using the name of some other person with whom you could have a better relationship.

Six

Managing Your Family

Charles Colson reached the top!

In the days before Watergate he was known as President Nixon's hatchet man—a blunt-speaking presidential aide with an impressive White House office, a six-figure income, a yacht, a limousine, and a chauffeur. Colson had marks of success that most of us only dream about—power, money, fame, status, access to the world's most important people.

He also had a "gnawing, inexplicable hollowness inside" that persisted during his rise to power. Years after Watergate, Colson spoke to a commencement audience at Taylor University and looked back over his life. He talked about his fall from power, his time in the penitentiary, his conversion to Christianity, his present work, and his accomplishments. "The real legacy of my life is not my achievements, but the fact I was a convict, a fallen political leader who went to prison."

Since his release over a decade ago, Charles Colson has devoted himself to writing, speaking, and work in United States prisons. Along the way, the former White House aide has established himself as one of our keenest social critics. His perceptive commencement address, for example, showed that Colson has considerable insight into the thinking of modern young people.

Yuppie Mentality

Two or three decades ago, masses of angry college-age radicals were rising in rebellion against the established values and materialistic business practices of the West. Now all of this has changed. The post-Watergate era has given birth to a generation known as yuppies—young urban professionals, mostly in their twenties and thirties, most part of the "baby boom" that followed World War II. These are hard-working people who know the value of education and who strive for excellence. They have high goals, affluent life-styles, and dedication to their careers.

From Charles Colson's experienced perspective, yuppies also have values and assumptions that are harmful and self-destructive. "My life was the American dream fulfilled, the envy of today's most zealous yuppie," Colson stated in his commencement speech. "I embodied the truth of what someone once wrote: The poor are better off than the rich because they still think money will buy happiness, while the rich know better."

Today's young adults have not heard that message. Many of their lives are ruled by self-absorption, the building of careers, and the pursuit of possessions. This is the first generation to be raised in a television era, and modern young adults want what the media have promised: lives that are relatively problem-free, professional power, self-esteem through affluence, freedom to "do your own thing," and the ability to have life's pleasures now—without waiting. This is a generation of fast-moving, impatient people who don't want to be bothered by political realities. "Nuclear war?" says one bumper sticker on a new BMW, "What about my career?"

It is difficult to live in Western society and not be influenced by the values that many (but not all) younger people so enthusiastically seek. Regardless of your age in years or your place in life, you might agree that a little of the yuppie mentality is in most of us.

Life for many people is a pursuit of pleasure, prosperity, possessions, power, and positions of prominence. We have become experts in managing our careers. We have learned how to dress for success. We know how to manage money and control time.

But we don't know how to control our kids.

We have trouble managing our marriages.

Our personal lives are sometimes in shambles.

Yuppie Marriage

Shirley Zussman is a psychotherapist in Manhattan and former president of the American Association of Sex Educators, Counselors, and Therapists. Her clients, mostly successful young couples, have disintegrating marriages and dull sex lives. Driven by the pressures, long hours, and constant demands of their careers, these two-paycheck couples have little time left for building intimate, loving marriages. Many are "too pooped for passion." For many, says therapist Zussman, there is "little or no time for sex." Physical intimacy has become one more thing they have to work into an already hectic schedule.

For those with children, and especially for parents without partners, the pace can be even faster and the schedules tighter. It takes time, energy, and patience to nurture an intimate relationship, to build a successful marriage, and to create a caring family. It isn't easy—some would say it isn't possible—to successfully manage both our careers and our families.

But there is hope.

Strong and Healthy Families

Numerous books and articles have told us what's wrong with modern families, but Dr. Nick Stinnett from the University of Nebraska wanted to know what is good about the family. In an impressive study of family strengths, his research team contacted three thousand families from North and South America, Europe, and South Africa. Most responded to questionnaires and a few hundred, in addition, were interviewed in depth. Strong families from both rural and urban areas; strong black and white families; strong Jewish, Polish, and Italian families; strong wealthy, middle-income, and poor families; strong single-parent families— all were included in proportions roughly equivalent to the societies from which they came.

Families and Nations

Why was this project done? In a recent speech Stinnett noted that ancient Egypt, Rome, Greece, and other great civilizations came to the peak of their power when families were strong. In each of these cultures . . .

> The family was important. Family members cooperated with one another. They interacted with one another. They depended on each other.
> Then as these nations progressed along their path of destiny, the family came to be not so highly valued, the culture became extremely individualistic. It was a "do your own thing" philosophy to an excessive degree. The families deteriorated. When that happened the societies themselves fell. . . .

I think each of us knows deep inside that so much of our happiness, so much of our emotional well-being depends on or is influenced to a great degree by the quality of the human relationships we have, and particularly by the quality of those intimate relationships we call family relationships. So promoting family strengths should be one of our country's top priorities.[1]

Qualities of Healthy Families

Their investigation of family strengths led Stinnett and his colleagues to a remarkable conclusion. Despite the great diversity of families in the study, several qualities emerged that were common to them all. Strong, healthy, happy families all had good family communication, spent time together, were committed to the family group, showed appreciation for one another, were able to solve problems in times of crisis, and had some kind of religious commitment.

The first of these—good communication—was discussed in the previous chapter. In strong families, the people talk to one another, try to understand one another, respect one another, and listen carefully.

This does not mean they always agree. Sometimes family members get mad at one another and express their feelings freely. To some extent this could be one reason why they get along so well. Conflicts are in the open. The arguments focus on issues and the family members don't spend their time attacking one another's character traits or tearing one another down as persons.

In healthy families there is banter, joking, and superficial conversation as well as discussion of deeper, more serious topics. Undoubtedly there is also avoidance of the communication traps that we discussed in chapter 5.

If you want to manage your marriage and your family, you must learn to communicate.

Successful Families Spend Time Together

Good communication and family intimacy won't come unless you spend time together.

In his seminars, Dr. Stinnett sometimes asks people to close their eyes, relax, and think for a few minutes about their happiest childhood memories. You may want to do this before you read further.

If you are like most people, your memories go back to family times. These may not have been major events. A picnic, going to grandmother's house, listening to bedtime stories—these are the kinds of things we remember fondly. On hot summer days, my grandfather used to take me on long afternoon walks to a park near the lake. We would wander by the flowers, look at the caged parrots, and sometimes splurge on a nickel ice-cream cone. They were happy relaxed times; just the two of us—together.

The Nebraska researchers found that togetherness in happy families doesn't just come by itself. Families make it happen. They look for times of interaction and work this into their busy schedules.

Is this becoming increasingly rare in our society? Yuppies aren't the only ones with busy, pressured lives. Many teenagers have schedules so full of school, friends, part-time jobs, television, and extracurricular activities that there is little time to sleep and no part of life left for the family. Busy homemakers, career-building parents, pressured students, overextended grade-school kids—all of us are busy, and the family suffers as a result.

How then can we find time to be together?

• Decide whether or not your spouse and family are important—important enough to take some of your time and energy.

- Determine to make time for your mate and your family. For many of us this means writing "family time" into our schedules.
- Discuss all of this with other family members. If you try to impose a family-togetherness program, somebody is likely to balk. Try, instead, to get most or all of the family to discuss and agree on a family-time plan.
- Don't make promises that you don't keep. There are times when work and other pressures make it necessary to cancel plans. But these times should be very rare. When you commit yourself to doing something together, follow through. This applies to promises made to your children, but it also applies to your spouse.
- Remember that children and adults have a different definition of *maybe* and *soon*. Have you ever told children, especially younger children, that *maybe* there can be a family vacation or visit to the circus? To the child that is a firm promise. Say you plan to do it *soon*, and the child takes this to mean "right now." When you make such statements and don't follow them with action, there can be great disappointment and anger.
- Set up some family dates. Family togetherness can be supplemented by quality husband–wife and parent–child "us-only" times together. I still enjoy "dates" with my wife and with each of my college-age daughters. Often we don't do anything expensive or spectacular. We go out for breakfast, do some shopping together, or take in a concert. One-on-one time alone with each other can be valuable family experiences.

The time together is what makes this important. Good family management won't come unless you are willing to invest time with your spouse and other family members.

Successful Family Members Are
Committed to One Another

When I was a teenager growing up in Canada, I had visions of becoming a professional photographer. My hero was Yousuf Karsh, the now-famous Armenian refugee who moved to Canada over fifty years ago, opened a small studio in the nation's capital, and came to be known as Karsh of Ottawa. He has photographed most of the world's famous people—Winston Churchill, Queen Elizabeth, Helen Keller, Rudolf Nureyev, Pope John Paul II, Albert Einstein, Leonid Brezhnev, George Bernard Shaw, and a modern "Who's Who" listing of others.

Perhaps it isn't surprising that Karsh is known as a perfectionist. He will spend ten or fifteen minutes rearranging lights a fraction of an inch to get the effect he wants. His patience is legendary; his dedication to the craft of portraiture has made his pictures famous all over the world. His is the kind of commitment that makes successful careers.

It is this commitment that also makes successful families.

Recently, a For Sale sign appeared on the lawn of a house not far from where we live. The people who live there have a son with a serious addiction to drugs. He grew up in a comfortable suburban neighborhood and a good home. Many of his peers have gone to college and probably will move into successful careers. He, instead, developed a hard-drug habit. In time, the family got him to a drug rehabilitation treatment center, but the costs were incredible.

To meet these expenses, everybody in the family worked harder. The parents, both professional business people, each took a morning paper route to earn extra money. When the bills kept piling up, the family decided to sell their house and move into a rented apartment.

I suppose there has been anger, discouragement, and frustration in that home, but there is also commitment. The parents refused to abandon their son. The family held together despite tremendous pressure, and the young man is now drug-free and working to build a new life.

Few of us are called to make these kinds of sacrifices, but happy and successful families are willing to work together. The family members have a firm commitment to one another and to the family group.

Commitment has been defined as a combination of determination plus effort. Without it, marriages and families aren't taken seriously. When the storms of life begin to howl, families without commitment tend to blow away. There is little to hold them together.

Is your marriage or family important enough to get your dedicated commitment? Are you willing to cross other things off your list to make time for the family? Does your life-style indicate that you tend to sacrifice your family on the altar of professional career advancement?

These are difficult and disturbing questions. They are questions that all of us must answer if we want to manage our marriages and families successfully.

Successful Families Express Appreciation

Near the beginning of this century, William James, the famous psychologist, wrote a book about human needs. It was widely read at the time, but years later the author commented that his manuscript had left something out. "I forgot one of the most important needs of all," he said, "the need to be appreciated."

Sometimes we are quick to see weaknesses in family members but are slow to show appreciation and give compliments. David Mace, a well-known marriage specialist, has stated that affirming one another is the basic glue that holds happy families together.[2] Dolores Curran would agree. In her study of healthy families, mutual affirmation and support came second on a list of fifty-six traits.[3] According to one of her informants, a pediatrician, "the best families I see are those in which members care enough about each other to give a sense of support and self-esteem. The kids know they're worthwhile because the family makes them worthwhile."[4]

A Three-Legged Stool

Many marriages begin with affectionate demonstrations of caring, consideration, and compliments. Nobody complains about being inconvenienced, and the couple is happily willing to share and help each other. Expressions of love and appreciation are common and flow freely.

Then things begin to change—often so slowly that nobody notices at first. Busyness and the pressures of life take over. Before long, the husband and wife forget to show the affection and appreciation that once were so natural and so frequent.

Like a three-legged stool, good marriages and healthy families need three supports if they are to stay upright and stable. These are core issues that build appreciation.

The first is **respect.** Even when you disagree or feel frustrated and hurt, try to remember that your spouse and family members are human beings with feelings and needs. Nothing is accomplished by embarrassing them, tearing them apart verbally, or refusing to forgive.

I once heard a young husband joke in public about his wife's weight. The comments were humorous and the audience howled with laughter, but the speaker's words said more about him than about his embarrassed wife. By showing insensitivity and disrespect for his spouse, the man was demonstrating his own lack of kindness, good manners, and caring.

Second, appreciation can be expressed more freely when there is **trust.**

Several years ago a scheduling mix-up made it necessary for me to stay overnight in a South American hotel. It was a beautiful place with comfortable accommodations and good food. Since I was traveling alone, I took a single room and settled down to spend some time reading.

About ten o'clock a seductively dressed woman appeared at my door. It didn't take long for me to discover what she wanted. Clearly a prostitute, she was ready to offer her services to the gringo who was alone in the hotel. When I refused to let her come in, my visitor looked surprised. She might have been even more amazed had she heard me tell my wife about the incident after I got home.

How does a wife respond to information like that? Mine appreciates the honesty. It shows we can trust each other to be faithful. That gives security and greater freedom to express appreciation.

Some families don't have that trust. One or more of the family members breaks the trust and becomes deceptive in hiding the truth. In time, others get suspicious and there are accusations and countercharges. Nobody in the family thinks any more about expressing appreciation.

In situations like this it would be foolish to ignore the actions of someone whom you don't trust or trust only partially. But you can still remain trustworthy yourself. You can show appreciation even when you must look long and hard to find something worth complimenting. Small actions like this do much to rebuild the trust that might be fading.

Giving is the third basis for building appreciation. Sometimes this means giving gifts, but more often you express yourself by giving compliments, time, energy, and attention. Givers may be inconvenienced, but how can you show appreciation if you are unwilling to give this any effort?

Practical Expressions of Appreciation

How do we express appreciation at home or elsewhere?[5]

• You can express appreciation by **words.** Look for opportunities to mention the positive traits and admirable behavior you see in another. If you have to raise something negative, surround this with positive comments. Say, for example, "You are normally a very caring person, but I think this one time. . . ."

• You can express appreciation by **writing.** Send notes through the mail, leave them around the house, tape them to the bathroom mirror, or slip them into the luggage of a family member who is leaving on a trip.

In our house, I'm usually the first one up and before doing much else I wander into the kitchen to make the coffee. Recently, I found a note in the coffeepot. My wife wanted to say thank-you for my coffee-making in the morning. Short little notes like that can do wonders to boost morale and strengthen family relationships.

• You can express appreciation by **listening** and sometimes by keeping quiet. Do you remember Job, the patient man who was suddenly besieged by a variety of life-changing problems? In the midst of his stress he didn't want to hear the chatter of a nagging wife. He was helped more by friends who came by, stuck with him, and said nothing. They showed their appreciation and caring by their presence.

• You can express appreciation by **touch.** There are cultural differences here, and some families—like some individuals—are uncomfortable with physical contact. But touches, hugs, and squeezes can be encouraging expressions of caring and appreciation.

• You can express appreciation by acts of **kindness, hospitality,** and **service.** This may involve helping one another—even without being asked—and not keeping records to see if everyone is contributing equally.

• You can express appreciation by **receiving** as well as by giving. What parent has not been moved by a child's drawing or other work of art that is presented with pride and delight? To receive such expressions with gratitude is a way to show appreciation to the giver.

If somebody compliments you, don't disagree with the compliment or shrug it off. A simple "Thank-you," or, "I appreciate that," encourages the other person. Accepting the compliment is a way you can show appreciation.

• You can express appreciation by **giving** one another **freedom to grow.** When we try to squelch creativity or hang on tightly to family members we give the message that dependency is all-important. As a husband and father, I show confidence in my wife and children whenever I encourage them to be creative or to develop their interests and potentialities. My encouragement shows that I appreciate their capabilities.

• You can express appreciation by **gentle confrontation.** The goal here is not to attack, but to point out some failure, weakness, annoying habit, or blind spot that the other person may be unwilling or unable to see. Try to do so gently, showing that you care enough to confront.

• You can express appreciation by **setting priorities.** Each family member, but especially parents, must ask where the family fits within his or her own set of priorities. It isn't very encouraging or affirming for a family to see that one or more of its members pushes the family into the background. Here is another place where actions speak louder than words.

• You can express appreciation by **prayer.** It is encouraging to know that others are praying for us and our needs. Even people who are not religious appreciate the fact that believers take the time and effort to pray for family members.

Successful Families Handle Crises Effectively

The Nebraska Family Strengths Study went on for several years. During that time, researchers found a lot of families who were facing crises. Those who coped effectively faced their crises head-on and tried to take action. Even when things were bad, strong families could see something positive in every situation, and they focused on that which was good.

John Baucom is a practicing clinical psychologist, former Marine Corps officer, Vietnam veteran, conference speaker, and consultant on human relations. He is a family man who almost didn't survive the crises of his own childhood. By the time he was ten, John Baucom's world had begun to fall apart. His parents had been separated and their divorce was near. His grades were dropping. His friends no longer came to visit. He argued with his sisters, his mother, and the grandparents with whom he lived. He wondered if the divorce was his fault and his ten-year-old mind saw no way out of a miserable situation.

One night there was a blur of activity in the living room: confusion, fear, screaming, crying, and the explosive sound of a gunshot. John's father lay dead in a pool of blood. Nobody noticed the ten-year-old boy who ran to the kitchen and grabbed a large butcher knife. "It seemed logical at the time," Dr. Baucom wrote later. "I would join my father and spend eternity with him. For some reason I felt no pain as the knife entered my side. A scream came from within me, although I didn't recognize my own voice. I recall my grandfather wrapping his strong arms around me. I began to sob almost convulsively as he held me to his chest. My body jerked as I slowly lost consciousness."[6]

John Baucom survived his family crisis and now devotes his life to helping others, especially suicidal teenagers, who face the crises of living.

Oh, No, Not This!

What does the word *crisis* bring to mind? Some may think about death in the family, severe illness, divorce, a job loss, a serious house fire, or the attempted suicide of some teenager. Crises like these are serious and disruptive. They put tremendous pressure on the family.

Some crises are less intense but these, too, can be disruptive. One writer has defined suffering as "anything that makes us think, 'Oh, no, not this!' "[7] I can't think of a better definition of a crisis. Healthy families learn how to cope without falling apart in the process.

• You can cope by facing the crisis honestly, discussing it within the family.

• You can cope by honestly sharing feelings. Most crises are accompanied by anxiety, anger, hurt, resentment, discouragement, and the kind of guilt that John Baucom felt when his parents prepared to divorce. To pretend that feelings do not exist only prolongs the crisis and makes adjustment longer and more difficult.

• You can cope by drawing closer to people who help. Stinnett and his research colleagues found strong families willing to accept the comfort, encouragement, and guidance that came from relatives, neighbors, and friends.[8] In this country we admire rugged individualism, but that doesn't help anybody in times of crisis. People need people, and families need support from other families.

• You can cope by trying to understand the situation. Some things about crises can never be understood clearly. After centuries of debate, philosophers and theologians still don't understand why people suffer or why bad things happen to good people. It helps to ponder these issues, however. It is valuable to think about what caused the crisis, to recognize that some things will never be changed (like the death of a mate) but that other things can be salvaged (like rebuilding a broken life or recovering from a heart attack). In all of this, understanding is clearer and coping is more effective when you talk over the situation with another person.

• You can cope by considering practical actions. Now that the crisis has occurred, what can you and your family do to handle the problem? What steps can you take (even small steps) to "pick up life" and go on living? What skills, abilities, or training do you have that will help you meet the crisis?

In planning like this, try not to spend time blaming yourself or others for the crisis. Don't sit around waiting for others to rescue you or to come up with solutions to your family problems. Even when the crisis has come from situations beyond your control, think about the things you could do to cope. That may include taking specific action. It probably will also involve a change in your attitude and an effort to see things in as positive a perspective as possible.

• You can cope by prayer. Almost all of the healthy families in the Nebraska study turned to religion in their times of crises. Ask God to give you peace, wisdom, and guidance. Don't forget the comfort that comes from others who believe as you do and from spiritual leaders in your community.

• You can cope by reaching out to others. At first, this may be difficult, but often the best way to help yourself is to help others. This lets you keep a realistic perspective on your problems, it prevents you from moping about your difficulties, and it is good therapy both for you and for the people you help. If you wonder about this, consider Alcoholics Anonymous. AA members are models of people who help others, and help themselves in the process.

Successful Families Tend to Be Religious

For many years, Pat Williams was general manager of the world champion Philadelphia 76ers basketball team. His wife, Jill, was a former beauty queen, a talented entertainer, and a gracious hostess who one day announced that she was walking out of their beautiful home and ten-year marriage, taking the children with her.

The problem was not infidelity, mate beating, or family violence. None of these existed. But the marriage had grown stone-cold because of unrealistic expectations, lack of communication, insensitivity, and life-styles that were too busy with other things.

The Williamses wrote a book about their marriage and described how, in time, it was rekindled with principles similar to the ones discussed in this chapter.[9] The couple had to rebuild their broken-down communication. Pat Williams had to reevaluate his priorities, his neglect of the family that had come with the pursuit of a career, his driven life-style, and his failure to show the sensitive caring that every family member needs. Jill Williams was willing to be honest about her anger, her feelings of insecurity and rejection, her depression.

Stories of marital neglect and breakup are common today, but few divorcing couples are as religious as Pat and Jill Williams. Why didn't their religion keep them from having problems?

No amount of religious faith will blot out the tensions that come when husbands and wives take each other for granted, ignore their families, and get swept up in self-centered activities. Even when there are problems, however, marriages and families are more inclined to survive and grow when there is strong belief in God, regular attendance at religious services, and family prayer or Bible reading. Jill and Pat Williams saw this in their marriage; Nick Stinnett discovered it in his research.

The religion that strengthens families is not the casual, largely meaningless ritual that almost all families go through on occasion. Happy, strong families take their beliefs seriously, believe that God is interested in their lives, and think of religion as something personal and practical.

Don't assume that belief in God is necessary for family stability. Many nonreligious people have families that are strong; in contrast, some religious families are weak. In general, however, families that pray together do stay together. These families are happy together and devoted to the kinds of values that bring success in all areas of life—love, tolerance, kindness, support, and concern for others.

Traits of a Healthy Family

Dolores Curran would not claim to be a scientist. She is better known as an educator, writer, and columnist who maintains a strong interest in the family.

Around the time those University of Nebraska researchers were doing their carefully designed scientific analysis of families, Curran decided to do an informal study of her own. In an effort to discover what makes families healthy, she sent 500 questionnaires to teachers, pastors, pediatricians, social workers, counselors, leaders of volunteer workers, and others who work with families. To her amazement, 501 questionnaires came back.

In her book, *Traits of a Healthy Family*, Curran lists the fifteen characteristics that were mentioned most often. They are reproduced as part of the questionnaire that follows this chapter. You may want to use this to help evaluate your own family.

It is easier to get your life out of neutral when your marriage and family are strong and healthy.

Managing Your Marriage and Family

This questionnaire is designed to apply both to marriages and to families. If you have children in your home, think about your family when you complete the questionnaire. If you have no children, think about your marriage.

Part One

Dolores Curran identified the following traits of a healthy family and reported them in her book *Traits of a Healthy Family*. (Minneapolis: Harper & Row, 1983. The following list is reproduced with the author's permission.)

1. As you read the list, think of your own marriage or family. In the blank spaces on the left, write:

   5 if this trait is *almost always true* in your home
   4 if this trait is *often true* in your home
   3 if this trait is *sometimes true* in your home
   2 if this trait is only *occasionally true* in your home
   1 if this trait is *never true* in your home

According to the Curran research, the healthy family:

   _____ communicates and listens
   _____ affirms and supports one another
   _____ teaches respect for others
   _____ develops a sense of trust
   _____ has a sense of play and humor
   _____ exhibits a sense of shared responsibility
   _____ teaches a sense of right and wrong
   _____ has a strong sense of family in which rituals
         and traditions abound

_____ has a balance of interaction among members
_____ has a shared religious core
_____ respects the privacy of one another
_____ values service to others
_____ fosters table time and conversation
_____ shares leisure time
_____ admits to and seeks help with problems

Part Two

1. If you want to do so, you can total your score on this test. Totals range from 15 to 75. This is not a scientific measure, but higher scores indicate healthy family relationships.

2. Look at all of the items marked 1, 2, or 3. How could you work on these issues to improve your family? Write some specific suggestions below. _____

_____

_____

_____

3. What will you do first?_____

_____

_____

Seven

Managing

Your

Career

She's been called a "show-biz matriarch," "remarkably talented," "one of the nicest, most congenial people in the business."

She first starred in *South Pacific*, worked with Gordon MacRae in *Oklahoma*, teamed up with Robert Preston in *Music Man*, and won an Academy Award for her role in *Elmer Gantry*. She was known in thousands of households as the musical mother of television's top-rated "Partridge Family."

In real life, Shirley Jones has always been part of show business. Her stepson, David, and son, Shaun Cassidy, became stars on their own, but not before they saw their father fail in his own struggles to reach the top.

In an interview on a Hollywood film set, Shirley Jones talked about her late husband, Jack Cassidy. "Jack was never secure," she began. "Poor Jack worked so hard, and he never felt the business did right by him. He always felt the brass ring was there, but he never caught it. He became very bitter and frustrated. . . .

"He had talent, yes—drama, singing; Jack was New York, he was Broadway. People said he looked like John Barrymore, which he did. It used to kill him that so many mediocre talents and no-talents rose to the top. It's really insane who makes it and who doesn't."[1]

Have you ever felt like that? Have you worked hard to build a career and watched as others have forged ahead for no explainable reason? Have you struggled, like Jack Cassidy, with bitterness and frustration because the brass ring of success seems to elude you?

Worn Down by the Daily Grind

When we fail to get the success we want, many of us work harder, put in more hours, or try more diligently to please the boss. Even at the beginning of our careers we can become what Gordon MacDonald has called "driven people."[2] Read the following checklist and ask how many of these apply to you:

Driven people are

—greatly concerned about accomplishments and strive for more and more achievements;

—preoccupied with the symbols of success, including titles, privileges, and awards;

—caught in the uncontrolled pursuit of something bigger; these people are constantly restless in their search for more efficiency, greater results, and deeper experiences;

—more concerned about succeeding than about integrity, kindness, sensitivity to people, or getting along with others;

—highly competitive, driven to win;

—often filled with anger that frequently is hidden but tends to surface when things aren't going well; and

—abnormally busy, seeking to make every minute count. There is little time for rest or reflection. Work goes on at a hectic pace, month after month.

Driven people don't always see that they are driven. Some fail to notice (or admit) success when it does come and many take no pleasure in their accomplishments. Instead, these people keep pushing, often with little joy, vitality, or inner peace. Eventually, their bodies collapse, their marriages fail, or they fall into periods of depression and self-doubt.

Insurance companies report an increase of claims from people who blame their jobs for creating severe anxiety, chronic depression, nervous breakdowns, and other stress-related problems. Many do have boring jobs, unreasonable supervisors, unpleasant work associates, incompetent colleagues, inconvenient hours, and continual demands. The stresses can be even greater for driven people with their self-imposed standards and pressures to succeed. It is easy for any of us to be worn down by the daily grind.[3]

But this doesn't have to happen. There are ways to manage your career more effectively, ways that depend somewhat on others, but mostly on you.

Career Management Depends, in Part, on Circumstances

Sister Marijane Ryan must have needed time to adjust when she left her Irish Catholic roots in Boston and was sent to a small Arizona town to care for a nun dying of cancer. During those long, hot days, Sister Ryan made friends with some local children, including a six-year-old

Navajo boy whose polio had left him unable to walk. Could he be helped?

Every morning, the nun from Boston slipped into cowboy boots under her long habit, moved outside, and worked at teaching the boy how to walk. Every morning the Navajo medicine man—who had noticed these therapy sessions—would arrive in his horse-drawn wagon, park under the shade of a nearby tree, and watch.

"The boy tried to teach me Navajo, and I tried to speak to the medicine man," Sister Ryan said later. "But I could never get any reaction out of him."

One day, after four months of patient therapy, the boy stood by himself between two chairs. And the medicine man noticed.

Suddenly he took off with his horse and wagon, but soon he was back, with his three-year-old grandson, a victim of cerebral palsy. Three weeks later Sister Ryan had fifteen children—the first of over six hundred physically and emotionally handicapped youngsters who have been helped by what is known now as the St. Michaels Association for Special Education.[4]

When she moved from Boston, Sister Ryan had no plans to start a school, no inner drive to achieve success and accomplishment, no list of five- and ten-year career goals to guide her work, no longing for the praise that has capped her efforts. She saw a need, responded to circumstances, trained the Navajos to operate the clinic, and later went on to other work.

This isn't the usual story of vocational success, but it illustrates the principle that circumstances often influence the directions of our careers.

This idea goes against most of the enthusiastic promises in self-help books. Everybody knows that successful careers often are molded by the planning, preparation, determination, and consistent efforts of individual men and women who persist, in spite of obstacles, and go on to reach the top. At the same time we must recognize that circumstances also have a bearing on our careers.

In describing her show business family, Shirley Jones noted that "packaging is the way it's done." One of her sons is talented but still uncertain about a career choice. Even if he didn't have talent, the actress suggested, "he and I are both aware he'd still get offered a million dollars to go out and perform on his name alone."[5] Maybe that isn't fair, but it's often the way things are. This is a reality that must be accepted if we hope to manage our careers, and our lives, with success.

Ain't It Awful

In his best-seller *Games People Play* psychiatrist Eric Berne described what he called the "Ain't It Awful" game.[6] People with this mind-set react to adverse circumstances by sitting back, doing nothing, and talking freely about the awful injustices of life. These are the people who bemoan their lack of education, abilities, or physical capabilities. They complain about their lack of opportunities and explain why others get the breaks.

Such talk accomplishes nothing. It is far better to accept the circumstances of life, do the best we can despite setbacks, and keep plugging. Comedian Rich Hall stated this concisely when he was asked about his own career. "Don't compare yourself to others," he responded. "Do the best that you can with whatever is thrown your way and take the opportunities that come along."[7] Most people who think like this soon learn that life's circumstances and adversities can be motivating. They can strengthen us, teach us, and give wisdom that helps when we try next time.

Careers, like life, aren't entirely under our own control. We can't always control circumstances but we can deal with attitudes and the ways we react to circumstances. That's an important way to win at life-management.

Career Management Depends, in Part, on Your Values

Several years ago, actress Sissy Spacek appeared as the main character in an Emmy-nominated film, *Verna: USO Girl.* Verna was a clumsy song-and-dance girl, hired by a USO troupe because nobody else was available. She sang off-key and didn't dance very well, but Verna was convinced she was destined for stardom. She was sure that thousands would attend her funeral when she died, and her fame as a performer would be immortalized forever.

Verna's performances got bad reviews but she did make a hit with one soldier. He wanted to marry her, but Verna was unwilling to disrupt her career. She kept singing, even when circumstances were dangerous. She ignored the critics and refused to heed those who urged her to go back to that caring GI.

One night, Verna's career was abruptly terminated by a land mine. An Army Public Relations Officer heard about the first USO girl to die in action and decided her story could be a good morale booster. He arranged a funeral. Some foreign dignitaries attended, and Verna's casket was followed by a band.

Nobody remembered her name. Nobody knew she had rejected love, driven herself to get success, and died with neither.

But she did have a big funeral.[8]

The Marks of Success

How do you define success? When you get to the end of your life what would you like to have accomplished?

Most people think of success in terms of achievements, money, power, prominence, and all the trappings of affluence. For many, success means fulfillment, "doing your own thing," enjoying your work, having freedom, and being happy. In a society that values speed, efficiency, and convenience, many want success to come quickly. We aren't much motivated by stories of people who take forever to get to the top. We aren't too interested in hearing about people who died before their accomplishments were noticed.

Still we can learn from the life of Gregor Mendel, the Austrian monk who discovered the principles of heredity. He failed his teacher's examinations three times but continued with his biological work nevertheless. Over a period of ten years, he crossbred twenty-one thousand plants, kept careful records of his findings, and unlocked the secrets of genetics. Nobody in the scientific community paid any attention until well after his death.

Was Mendel successful? What about Shirley Jones, Jack Cassidy, Sister Ryan, or Verna the USO girl? What about you?

Motivational expert Denis Waitley believes that lasting and satisfying success comes to those who are willing to persist in doing things that most of the population doesn't want to do.[9] Success usually comes slowly. It comes most often to those who patiently strive for quality in their work, and it often comes without the trappings of fame and money.

Does success bring security and satisfaction? Entertainer Jimmy Dean would say no. From his perspective, only fools are satisfied. Fran Tarkenton would agree. The former football star, who now heads a management consulting firm in Atlanta, once wrote about success and job satisfaction:

> It seems to me that it is precisely the ability not to be satisfied that keeps us going and produces high performance and achievement. If you were truly satisfied, I think you would

reduce your effort to achieve. I know *I have worked my hardest when I was most dissatisfied, with a goal clearly in mind that I felt I had to achieve....*

I can remember times when I began a football game feeling very satisfied with myself. I may have had several good games in previous weeks and was confident that I was performing well, was being recognized and respected for my performance, and knew that my teammates and I had the skill to outperform our opponents. I remember being defeated by lesser teams when I had that exact frame of mind. I was satisfied. I think I have played my best games when I was least satisfied, hungry to prove myself. I think this is why some of the best teams in football are beaten by some of the worst. The lesser team is hungry, angry and determined. The better team is satisfied. The better team loses![10]

Why Is Success So Important?

Why do some people drive themselves to be successful, even when they already have fame and fortune? Why do others, like Gregor Mendel, work long hours even when they get no acclaim and appear to be having little success? Why do students push to boost their grades or young athletes torture their bodies in preparation for some sports competition? Why do thousands of others drift all through life with little drive and no apparent urge to be successful? Why did Cézanne, the famous French painter, keep working almost to the time of his death, even though his worldwide reputation was already well established? His body was frail and sickly when the old artist was asked about life. "All I know," the famous man replied, "is that I've just got to go on painting."

There are no simple answers to questions about motivation. We all have our own reasons, sometimes unconscious and unrecognized, for doing the things we do.

In Western society, however, many seem to have slipped into a mind-set that cannot separate what we *are* from what we *do.* This is the belief that you aren't worth much unless you succeed in accomplishing something. In hundreds of subtle ways we tell our children, and ourselves, "If you aren't good at something, then you really are good for nothing." Failure to achieve is taken as a personal slap in the face; a clear proof that you really don't count and really aren't worth much.

This kind of thinking lodges in the mind, pushes many to keep working, and becomes a firmly held value.

What Do We Mean by Values?

The word *values* refers to those beliefs that you consider to be really important in life. Values can have a powerful influence on your career and self-management.

In his study of peak performers, Charles Garfield found that successful people have a strong commitment to their values. These high achievers believe in the importance of:

- Accomplishment—getting things done efficiently and well;
- Contributions—doing something worthwhile, often something that is helpful to others;
- Self-development—learning to manage our lives;
- Creativity—taking risks and being innovative;
- Teamwork—doing things with others;
- Quality—a striving for excellence that includes the desire to get feedback and find ways to improve; and
- Opportunity—the chance to face and surmount new challenges.[11]

Values like these are important because *more than anything else, your values determine what you do and how you act.* If you value money and possessions, you are likely to work hard trying to become rich. If you value education, you will study hard and hope your kids do the same. If you accept the idea that people don't count for much unless they achieve, you are likely to strive for achievements. If you value other people and the alleviation of human suffering, you might become like Mother Teresa, who works sacrificially in the slums of Calcutta.

What are your values? Perhaps you haven't thought about this, but even unrecognized values can influence the way you manage your career.

Before you read further, you may want to turn to the values questionnaire at the end of this chapter. It is designed to help you think about the values that affect the management of your vocation.

Career Management Depends, in Part, on Your Interests and Abilities

Work, as we all know, is no challenge when a job is boring, uninteresting, too difficult, or too easy. There is little joy working in a place where nobody needs your skills or where the boss looks for abilities that you don't have.

How sad that many people go through life trapped in these kinds of jobs. Every morning they leave for work that is boring, nonfulfilling, and without any kind of challenge. For some this may be tolerated because they have never known anything different. Others have little ambition to change. They are like one of my former neighbors who has almost no education, no marketable skills, no initiative, no desire to do anything different, and no real hope that things will get better. I don't criticize this man; I feel sad when I think about his largely meaningless drift through life.

At times, all of us get locked into jobs that are less interesting and challenging than we would like. Effective career management can help you get out of these situations, but it is best if you have a clear idea of your interests and abilities.

Psychological tests can help you find these but you might prefer to do a little test of your own. Take a blank piece of paper and draw three columns.

At the top of the first column write: Interests—What I *like* to do.

At the top of the second column write: Abilities—What I *can* do.

At the top of the third column write: Concerns—What I would really *like to see changed* in this world.

Take some time to fill in the columns by jotting down your interests, abilities, and concerns. Discuss your conclusions with a friend who knows you well.

Now think about your present job. Does it provide interest, make use of your abilities, deal with the real concerns you have about life? What kind of work would suit you better? What extra training would you need to get such a job? What kind of work would give you the time and freedom to cultivate your interests, abilities, and concerns when you are off the job?

Your Career Odyssey

Madelon DeVoe Talley has been a successful Wall Street investor. She was a vice-president of the Dreyfus Corporation, director of investments for the State of New York, and managing director of Rothschild, Inc. Her book on career management describes some of her own struggles and successes, the advice she picked up from leading financial analysts in New York, and her guidelines for surviving in the cutthroat world of giant corporations.[12] Many of her suggestions apply to people who work far from corporate boardrooms.

It can be helpful, she suggests, to think about your own vocational journey or "odyssey." List all of your past vocational experiences. You might want to write these in three columns again: those that were successful, those that were neutral, those that were failures.

Then look at what you have written. What did you do best? Where did you fail? What things interested you most? By looking back, you sometimes can see patterns, interests, and directions that could be helpful for the future.

Reflecting on her own career, Madelon Talley discovered that:

1. Motivation is the key to success and effective career management. If you aren't motivated to succeed, you won't.

2. Flexibility and a willingness to take risks are marks of people who succeed. There are more dreamers than doers in this world because most people are afraid to take risks. Maybe this is what keeps many fields from being overrun with mediocrity.[13]

3. An inventory of your assets and liabilities is essential. A group of successful writers was recently asked to share the biggest hurdles of their careers. Their answers boiled down to this: "finding what I do best and having the sense to do it."[14] Try to discover what you do best and keep aware of your weaknesses. Successful people find jobs that maximize their assets but don't force them to draw too much on their personal weaknesses and liabilities.

4. Persistence, the determination and commitment to work toward a goal, is important for career management.

Lee Iacocca was fired after twenty years with the Ford Motor Company. It wasn't easy to face that rejection, but Iacocca spent a summer thinking about his strengths and weaknesses, pondering his interests and abilities, learning from a reflection on his own career odyssey. His subsequent rise to power at Chrysler and his fame throughout the world are well-known.

In her career-management book, Madelon DeVoe Talley pointed to Lee Iacocca as an example of someone who refused to be defeated by career setbacks. After months of work, Talley finished her manuscript and prepared to send it to the publisher. Then the unexpected happened.

Like Lee Iacocca, Madelon Talley was fired.

She read about it in the *New York Times*.

The lady who had written a book about career management was forced to apply its conclusions to herself.

In an epilogue to her book she wrote:

> Many people today choose, consciously or not, to stop dreaming or to ignore their dreams and to let things happen as they may. You see such people everywhere and they are easy to recognize. Sometimes they are wearing earphones, and for whatever private or musical reasons are keeping themselves oblivious to the world around them. . . . You see them in school, frittering away their time with superficialities. Later on, their wastefulness becomes even sadder.[15]

What about you, and me? When careers seem to go wrong do you stop dreaming and "let things happen as they may"? How do you avoid the frittering, superficialities, and wastefulness that could scuttle your own career? Taking the time to think about these questions can help with your career management and plans for the future.

Career Management Depends, in Part, on Your Goals

I got distracted recently.

I was leafing through books on career management and began noticing some of the helpful advice that successful people have shared.

"People remember you more by your big successes than by your big failures," states Bill Phillips, president of Ogilvy & Mather International.

"People who never take a chance, never get ahead," writes theologian Robert Schuller.

"Life is a self-fulfilling prophecy," suggests psychologist Denis Waitley. "You won't necessarily get what you want in life, but in the long run you will usually get what you expect."

"Six essential qualities are the key to success: sincerity, personal integrity, humility, courtesy, wisdom, charity," believes psychiatrist William Menninger.

"A strong liberal arts education is the key to career flexibility," claims John Sawyer, president of the Andrew Mellon Foundation.

"If you refuse criticism you will end in poverty and disgrace; if you accept criticism you are on the road to fame," said wise King Solomon in the Bible (Proverbs 13:18 TLB).

Words of advice like these can be challenging and encouraging. Sometimes I write them on little cards and tape them to places where they might be seen and remembered.

Nevertheless, even the most inspiring statements lose their power after a while. In managing a career, it would be foolish to ignore the advice and experiences of others, but ultimately you are the one who has to make decisions and determine the direction of your own career.

Self-Analysis—Doing a Career Audit

Determining your own career direction involves at least three tasks: *self-analysis* in which you do a career audit to take stock of your career right now; *self-monitoring* in which you determine your career goals and decide where you would like to be going; and *self-intervention*, the process of taking action to get what you want.[16]

It is never too early, or too late, to take a long, hard, honest look at your present career. This is what we mean by a *career audit*. It is a careful evaluation to determine where you have been, where you stand now, and where you would like to be going. It should be done every few years, but you probably will be most inclined to audit your career when you are getting started, feeling dissatisfied in your present work, looking for a new job, facing the questions of middle age, or looking ahead to retirement.

There is no set formula for auditing your career. The process involves thinking about your work, looking at your own skills and interests, and answering some thought-provoking questions. You may think of your own questions, but start with those in the career-audit questionnaire at the end of this chapter. Take the time to write out your answers and discuss them with one or two people who know you well.

Self-Monitoring

If you are independently wealthy, excessively lazy, well into retirement, or related to somebody with lots of money, you probably don't think much about work. The rest of us spend many hours on the job—whether we want to or not.

The planning ahead questionnaire at end of chapter 4 suggested that you think about your purposes in life and consider what you might like to be doing in five or ten years.

A similar analysis can apply to vocations. By now you probably are familiar with your basic values, interests, abilities, and concerns. You are learning what you do best and where you are less capable. You are realistic enough to know that some vocations will be closed to you—playing professional football, or being a concert pianist could be obvious examples—perhaps because you are too old, limited physically, lacking the needed talent and skills, or otherwise impeded by circumstances.

But many opportunities are still open, especially if you

are willing to plan carefully and take risks. You are not locked into your present career unless you think you are. Nevertheless, the sooner you move, the easier it is to make a change.

What do you want out of your work? What is the relative importance of working with people, machines, numbers, or business associates? How important are job security, income, freedom to set your own schedule, and the other issues listed in the career-audit questionnaire?

Think of some careers that would interest and satisfy you. Find out what you would need to do to enter these vocational areas.

It can be helpful to write down your career goals. The best goals are specific, realistic, practical, feasible, achievable in a certain time span, and measurable—so you can tell when the goals are reached. Each goal is most likely to be reached when you work out a series of smaller goals to help you progress, one step at a time.

Gwen Philips is a middle-aged lady whose children are grown and whose husband is involved in a successful restaurant business. Gwen has always wanted to be a counselor, but she lacked the training and never had opportunity to enroll in college classes.

Until recently.

A few years ago she did a career audit, looked at her interests and abilities, and wrote out some career goals. She knew education was essential so she began moving toward her ultimate goal by taking the first step—enrolling in a local junior college where she took classes alongside her nineteen-year-old daughter. Eventually Gwen got her B.A. in psychology and volunteered in a home for unwed mothers.

Going to graduate school seemed out of the question until she discovered a program that would let her get a Ph.D. by doing independent work, supervised by professional counselors in her hometown. Sometimes Gwen has to take short-term intensive courses at the university campus, but these times away from home are brief and her family is supportive. It will take a while, but Gwen will get a doctorate. Once she determined what to do, and how to move toward her goal, the biggest hurdle was taking the first step.

Self-Intervention

Many people spend hours fantasizing about the future, doing career audits, mulling over their good intentions—but never taking any action to get moving. Change, as we have seen, is risky. None of us wants to do anything foolhardy; it always is more comfortable to stay where we are. But that is no way to manage a career. Career management involves setting goals and moving toward them.

> **Career Management Depends, in Part, on a Balanced Life-Style**

You probably know people like them. Dan loves his family and spends time with them, but he always is so distracted with his work that he never really relaxes or enjoys himself. Van never takes time off. He hasn't had a vacation in several years because he always is too busy with the demands and challenges of his work. Jan combines her vacations with sales conferences and out-of-town business trips. This saves money and lets her combine business with pleasure.

All these people are successful and dedicated to their work, but each is bothered by disturbing problems. Dan is tense. He snaps at his kids and can't relax. Van has sleeping problems. His mind is always going and he's perpetually tired. Jan keeps getting headaches and takes too many painkillers. All three are showing signs of stress; each has let life become dominated by work.

It is possible to manage your career but to fail in controlling your leisure. One psychologist even suggests that the "cornerstone of life-style management" is learning to find a balance between your work and the nonwork parts of your life. Dan, Van, and Jan have let work contaminate the rest of life. Each needs to find a balance between achievement and success on one hand and satisfying involvements in leisure activities, hobbies, family, and friendships on the other.[17]

There are three ways to contaminate leisure with work.[18] The *leisure ruminators* are like Dan. They look like they take time off, but they really do not. Work is always in the back of their minds and it often slips into the conversation, even when they are supposedly relaxing. Van, in contrast, is a *leisure avoider*. He talks about the need for relaxation but he never quite gets around to taking time away—unless he feels himself sinking under the pressure and has to take a day or two off to get the strength to go back. Jan is a *leisure bender* who relaxes only when this can be done within the context of ongoing, work-related responsibilities. She goes to cookouts and cocktail parties but sees these as places to cultivate business contacts.

Does any of this describe you? Is it possible that your life-style could involve one, two, or even all three types of leisure contamination?

Decontaminating Your Leisure

Career management is most effective when we are able to develop life-styles that let us balance work with relaxation.

• Convince yourself that relaxation is important. Time away from work is more than a casual bonus to be fitted into your schedule if you feel so inclined. Leisure is a vital necessity if we are to maintain mental and physical health.

• Set aside regular time for relaxation. Make it a priority and give yourself enough time to do something different from your work.

• Decide what activities really help you relax. This may take time. For some it may mean sitting in the sun and resting. For others, it might involve activity, but try not to let this become goal directed, competitive, demanding, performance oriented. When that happens your relaxation isn't really relaxing.

• Expect to have difficulty slowing down. Some effective career managers have trouble adjusting to the idea that they should take time for meditation, recreation, diversion, and even a little loafing.

• Watch for greater efficiency, productivity, and inner calm that comes following time off. When there is balance between work and leisure, we end up doing better at both.

Keeping Things in Perspective

The paragraphs in this chapter almost all apply to me. Like so many others, I too struggle with career-management issues, encounter obstacles that interfere with my vocational goals, take periodic career audits, hesitate before taking risks, and strive to decontaminate my leisure time.

It helps for me to remember that life is short. Each of us is on this earth only for a while. I have interests, abilities, skills, values, and opportunities, but I won't keep going forever. My perspectives are not always perfect and my career decisions are not always right. Nevertheless, I move on, doing the best I can with the knowledge I have, supported by the family and friends I love and respect.

Can there be any better perspective on career management?

Values Questionnaire

Please fill in as many of the following blanks as you can.

Success

I would consider myself to be successful in life if:

1. _____
2. _____
3. _____

Satisfaction

I would be satisfied in my life and work if:

1. _____
2. _____
3. _____

Life Goals

If I had to list the three most important goals for my life, they would be:

1. _____
2. _____
3. _____

Personal Value

I would consider myself to be a valuable person if I:

1. _____
2. _____
3. _____

Money

If I had a million dollars, I'd spend it on:

1. _____

2. _____

3. _____

Time

The things I like best to do in my free time are:

1. _____

2. _____

3. _____

Future

If I had only six months to live, I would spend the time:

1. _____

2. _____

3. _____

These lists—dealing with your views of success, satisfaction, goals, personal value, money, time, and the future—can give you a pretty good view of what really is important in your life.

Please look over what you have written. How many of your answers are self-centered? Sometimes stress is harder to handle when too many of our values are self-centered.

There are no right or wrong answers to the above questions, but as you look over what you have written, do you want to make some changes in your life? How can you do this? Be specific.

Career Audit

Answer the following questions as honestly as you can. Write out your answers. Then share them with somebody who knows you well. Does the other person agree with what you have written?

1. List the things you like about your present job.
2. List the things you dislike about your present job.
3. List your major interests.
4. List the things you do best.
5. List your weaknesses.
6. What kinds of jobs have you refused in the past? Why?
7. What kinds of jobs have you accepted in the past? Why?
8. Which of your past jobs did you like most? Why?
9. Which of your past jobs did you like least? Why?
10. If there were no obstacles, and you could be in the ideal job, what would you be doing?
11. What would you have to do to get that kind of job?
12. What jobs are similar to the one you listed for question 10?
13. What would you have to do to get into these jobs?
14. If you changed careers, what would you gain and what would you have to give up?
15. Could you try out a new career for a while without quitting your present job? (Perhaps you could try something new on a part-time basis. If it works, you could shift to the new position full-time.)
16. Would you be willing to take a lower salary, lower status, or less convenient schedule in order to move to a new job or career?
17. Look at the following list. Please write:
    1 next to those items that are *very important* to you
    2 next to those items that are *important* to you
    3 next to those items that are *mildly important* to you

4 next to those items that are of *no importance* to you

_____ money

_____ personal satisfaction

_____ job security

_____ a job that is challenging

_____ a job that is fulfilling

_____ work that has variety

_____ flexibility of hours and location of work

_____ opportunities to learn new skills

_____ opportunities for advancement

_____ opportunities to be creative

_____ serving people

_____ prestige and status

_____ job autonomy—freedom to direct your own work

_____ managing other workers

_____ being my own boss

_____ variety within the job

_____ benefits—like health insurance, retirement funds, paid vacations, etc.

_____ Other (fill in the blanks)_____

18. Look over the above list. What are the three most important job characteristics for you?

19. Based on your answers to these questions, what action should you take to make changes in your career?

20. Make a note on a calendar or elsewhere reminding you to look over these questions again within the next couple of years.

Eight

Managing Your Resources

Louisa must have been a remarkable lady.

She was born on her father's thirty-third birthday, more than a century ago, and from him she learned the caring and compassion that shaped her entire life. In those days, when slavery was ingrained in American society, her teacher-father courageously admitted a black girl to his little school and was forced to close its doors as a result. When the family moved to Boston, Louisa and her three sisters saw their kindhearted father willingly take in abused wives and homeless children.

Regrettably, the father showed less sensitivity to his own family. Sometimes he went off on his own, looking for teaching jobs, while his wife and daughters were left to fend for themselves.

Much of this responsibility fell on Louisa. She taught school to bring in money. She struggled to keep some semblance of stability in the home when her younger sister died of scarlet fever, her father suffered a nervous breakdown, and her mother turned to Louisa for emotional support. "She chose to forego the fulfillment and security of marriage," her biographer wrote, so the family could have her undivided attention.

Once, when things had settled down for a while, Louisa enlisted as a nurse in the Union Army during the Civil War. The conditions were deplorable. Everything was unsanitary and Louisa was forced to exist on a diet of tea, potatoes, and rancid beef. Soon she contracted typhoid fever, developed mercury poisoning, and almost died.

Following a slow and painful period of recovery, Louisa turned to writing and attained fame as a novelist, but soon the family called again. The faithful daughter, now well into adulthood, nursed her mother until the elderly lady died. When another sister passed away, Louisa assumed responsibility for raising her young niece. The story saddened when Louisa's intellectual but impractical father got sick and needed his faithful daughter's continuing care.

She cared for him so well that she forgot to look after herself. On the day of his death, in the spring of 1888, Louisa caught a fatal cold. She and her father were eulogized two days later at the same funeral.

The caring lady from Massachusetts is not remembered today for her compassion or family devotion. She is better known, instead, as the author of two still-famous novels, based—some say—on the experiences of her own family. *Little Women* and *Little Men* were written by the caring lady whose full name was Louisa May Alcott.

A Nation of Advice

Did Louisa May Alcott ever think about time management? For a while, after her novels were published, she received considerable acclaim, traveled internationally, and saw substantial royalty checks. Did she worry then about the best ways to manage her money? Did she struggle to manage her energies and priorities so there would be time to write while she continued to manage her troubled family?

Life in those days was simpler than it is now, nearly a century after Louisa May Alcott's death. Bombarded by an avalanche of information, dazzled by radical and ever-changing technology, and bewildered by the increasing complexity of our society, we have become what one news magazine has called "a nation of advice."[1] Businesses, politicians, government agencies, and people like you and me look to experts who willingly give guidance on a variety of topics—often in exchange for a healthy fee. Seminars, workshops, talk shows, private consulting sessions, and a major share of the multibillion-dollar book-publishing industry are devoted to giving *how to* . . . instruction. The world today has more professional counselors than ever before, and the field of financial planning, barely alive in the 1960s, now employs over one hundred thousand highly paid practitioners.

Social scientists debate whether the advice does any good. Some complain that we are a nation obsessed with experts whose credentials, résumés, surveys, and fine-sounding language keep people from old-fashioned self-reliance. Many have noted that the advice industry is filled with smooth-talking phonies and frauds, some on radio and television, who lead people astray and do far more harm than good. Others wonder why some individuals are willing to get advice in public—like the woman who discussed her husband's extramarital affair with Phil Donahue while 7 million television viewers watched.

Life management is not easy. Things *do* change quickly and no one person can be an expert in everything. It is difficult to manage money, time, energies, families, educations, and personal crises. So we look for advisors and try to find people who have sensitivity, understanding, integrity, credentials, and relevant training.

Ultimately, however, the ball comes bouncing back to you and me. We make the decisions about what to do with our lives—including the ways we spend money and use time. In this chapter, we'll look at both of these.

Your Values Influence How You Spend Your Resources

"The love of money is the root of all evil . . ." (1 Timothy 6:10 KJV). That must be one of the most familiar quotations from the Bible—even though it often is misquoted by people who leave off the first three words. The biblical letter to the Hebrews gives similar advice: "Keep your lives free from the love of money and be content with what you have . . ." (Hebrews 13:5).

Advice like that isn't very popular. It goes against what most of us believe. We don't want to be content with what we have, even when we know that love of money can dominate our lives and put tremendous pressures on our families and careers. Compared with most people on this globe, we are rich, but this doesn't stop us from being concerned about financial issues, planning for the things we want to get, and thinking a lot about money.

Much of this thinking is influenced by three common attitudes: impatience, insecurity, and indulgence.

Impatience

How many times have you been urged to "buy now—pay later"? Advertisers make frequent reference to "easy terms," "low interest rates," and "instant credit." Only mothers of little children (sometimes with purses full of credit cards) talk about "saving up your money to buy what you want." The rest of us are more inclined to use "plastic money" to buy now and worry about paying at some more convenient time. Even the government works on the principle of borrowing from the future to pay for the present. As a result, governments and individuals both get further and further in debt.

Installment buying isn't always bad. We all purchase homes on the installment plan, and few people can pay cash for a new car. Most of us discover, however, that the buy-now-pay-later philosophy can quickly lead to big bills and financial pressures. We get impatient. We want to have things now. So we charge our purchases and go further into debt.

To avoid this problem, it helps to resist impulse buying, careless buying, and unbudgeted buying.

• *Impulse buying* often occurs at the checkout counter where the store manager displays all kinds of magazines, goodies, and gimmicks that you weren't planning to purchase. As a good money-saving policy, never buy anything on impulse—including those items displayed near the checkout counter. It is too easy to spend extra dollars on things we don't really need.

• *Careless buying* involves purchasing what you want or need without checking on quality. The toaster breaks down, you need a new one, so you slip into a store and buy what's available without bothering to check whether your selection is good. Someplace in the recesses of the mind we have the idea that if this one breaks down we can always return it, or get another. This kind of buying is convenient but it doesn't involve good money management.

• *Unbudgeted buying* comes when you make a purchase without thinking ahead. A few extra dollars on the Visa card seems so insignificant when you sign the bill, but how easy it is to discover, at month's end, that expenses have been climbing faster than income. Financial advisors tell you to plan ahead, keep records of how you spend money, and record where it is going. Most of us know this, but we don't think about it when a new sale is announced or something desirable is made available "on easy credit."

Many successful business people diligently handle large company budgets but make these impatience mistakes when handling their own personal and family finances.

Insecurity

Do people still spend money to impress the neighbors, "keep up with the Joneses," boost self-esteem, or avoid somebody's criticism? Probably you don't like to admit that social pressure influences your spending, but for most of us this still happens.

Almost ten years ago, our family moved into a new house in a suburban subdivision. Ours was one of the first homes to be built, and for several years our property was surrounded by fields of wildflowers, tall grass, and uncontrolled growths of weeds. We kept our lawn trim and neat but we enjoyed our rustic surroundings.

Then the fields began to fill up with houses. Many are larger than ours. They have manicured lawns, professional landscaping, and impressive, flower-lined driveways. Now I'm beginning to feel self-imposed pressure to clean out some of the brush near my property and to plant additional bushes and flowers.

This isn't necessarily bad. Additional landscaping will make my house look better and may increase the property value. I must be careful, however, not to let the subtle influence of social pressure trigger my own insecurities and cause me to spend unwisely.

Recently, one of my friends was appointed dean of the graduate school of psychology in the university where he teaches. Immediately he bought a new sports car. He didn't need it, he probably couldn't really afford it, and the people in his department weren't impressed by it. Was the purchase an attempt to keep up with the other deans and department chairmen? Was my friend trying to advertise his new status? Was he trying to make up for his own feelings of insecurity?

The basis of most insecurity is fear. We are afraid of not being accepted by others. We fear not having enough for our old age, for the education of our children, for the luxuries we might like in the future. As a result, we store up money and possessions like busy squirrels that stash away nuts for the winter. If we aren't careful, our lives are controlled by the desire for possessions. Financial burdens increase and the joy of living is squelched by that root of all evil—the love of money.

Indulgence

My friend with the sports car may have wanted only to indulge himself; to reward his own professional success. Probably that won't do any harm unless he falls into the "spend it while you've got it" mentality that characterizes many self-indulgent people.

These are individuals who live for the present and don't think much about the future. When they get money they spend it, without giving much thought to wise money management. Recently, a man who had won a million dollars in a lottery, had no money to pay a minor parking fine one year later. "I don't know where it all went," he told a reporter. "It just disappeared."

This man lived and spent in accordance with his priorities and values. We all do the same, even when we handle our money more responsibly. To manage resources well, and keep what we have from "just disappearing," each of us has to be aware of his or her own values and attitudes about spending.

Someone has said that the best way to find what a person really values is to look at how he or she spends money and uses time. Look at your checkbook sometime. After you pay necessary expenses like taxes, where does your money go? Think about the ways you spend your time—especially when you aren't working. Where does your time go? We tend to spend money and time on the things that are really important. Values control the management of our resources.

Good Resource Management Starts With Accurate Information

Glancing at a checkbook or thinking about how you spent time last week may be too casual and inaccurate to be of real help in self-management. To get control of runaway spending and lost time, we need to keep more accurate records.

Start with your money. It takes a little effort, but try to keep a record of how your money is being spent. You may only want to do this for a short period, but ideally it is best to keep records for a whole month.

On a paper that you keep at home, write down your major expenses—rent or mortgage, car payment, insurance, and other fixed costs. If you pay by check, you can get the information from your checkbook.

Then, start recording everything you spend. Carry a little notebook that easily slips into a pocket. What do you spend in the clothes store, the supermarket, the coffee shop? Don't forget to record gasoline, entertainment, telephone calls—everything. If you forget to record something, write down a good guess for what you spent, but recognize that the more accurate the records, the more helpful they will be.

At the end of the month, do some tallying. Where did your money go? Most of us are surprised at the answers. Is this how you want to spend your money?

A Money Autobiography

In one of my counseling courses, I require students to write a personal autobiography. The people who try hardest to talk me out of this assignment often discover that it can be very helpful. It lets beginning counselors understand themselves and see how their past experiences can influence their actions and thinking now.

Could something similar be done with money management? Take an hour or two sometime and write a money autobiography. What are your earliest memories about money? What are some happy and unhappy memories concerning money? What did you learn from your parents' attitudes toward money? What is your attitude now? Do you feel rich or poor, stingy or generous, worried about money or relaxed? What have you done with your money in the past? Have you given any away (apart from what you "give" to the government)? Do you spend it mostly on yourself? Do you handle money carefully, take risks, gamble, buy things that are expensive or not needed, use credit cards, try to keep up with somebody else's expectations?[2]

Writing answers to questions like these can help you understand your attitudes, values, and feelings about money. Some people in money-management groups have been courageous enough to share their money autobiographies. You might prefer to talk about this with someone whom you trust and know well. The feedback from others can be helpful as you move to get better control of your own money.

Where Does Your Time Go?

Keeping records about time can be as helpful as your records about money. In both cases, careful record keeping takes effort.

Recently a group of Australians was asked to keep an account of how they spent one twenty-four-hour time period. Everybody agreed to do this but many didn't quite get it done. Can you guess why? "We were too busy," most of them said. "We didn't have enough time."[3]

According to one survey, four out of five people in societies like ours feel regularly rushed for time.[4] We see it in our own lives and in the way we talk about time. "Time flies," we say.

"I did it in the nick of time."

"Time marches on."

"We don't have much time."

"Time's a-wasting."

We talk about borrowed time, working against time, and making the best use of time, but we rarely complain about having time on our hands or about time standing still.

Near the door of a high school classroom there hangs a plaque with these words: "Moments are golden opportunities. Are you throwing away your gold?" This little slogan reminded students to be time-conscious. But we can also be time-pressured; too much aware of time.

What happens to the 168 hours in your week? Do you know? Most of us can only guess how we spend our time. If you keep more accurate records you might be genuinely surprised.

Recently I decided to keep a tally of the hours I spend writing. Whenever I turn on the computer, I jot down the time, but am careful to deduct the minutes spent talking on the telephone, looking at the mail, getting another cup of coffee, gazing at the bird feeder near the window, or otherwise getting distracted. These digressions may be rejuvenating, but it is easy to get to the end of my writing day and discover that more time was spent digressing than working. Huge amounts of time had been wasted—when I thought I was working.

Some time-management books provide charts and graphs for recording how we spend our time. A plain piece of paper or a little notebook can do just as well. Try to keep a record for one or two somewhat typical weeks.

When you are done, tally your results. Are you surprised? How are you really spending your time? Are you satisfied with what you have discovered?

Before you start on this project let me suggest that you not try to keep a record of your time and money uses during the same week. You are more likely to stick with the task if you focus on one record, then do the other.

Good Money Management Involves Careful Planning and Self-Control

A local radio station used to carry a program on financial planning. Twice every day, a man with a mournful voice would answer listeners' questions about money and financial planning.

One morning, I read in the newspaper that our local financial advisor had been arrested. He was charged with fraud and several other financially illegal practices that had lined his own pockets but left some of his advisees a lot poorer. It came as no surprise when the radio station quietly dropped his program.

Finding a Reputable Financial Planner

In many places, laws are being passed to protect the public from incompetent financial planners, but many of these people still exist. Some have limited experience and little expertise, but they offer "financial planning services," sometimes from impressive offices that hide their ignorance.

How do we find competent advisors? Try to find someone with established credentials and a good reputation in the community. Avoid planners who have a vested interest in your money. These people may be honest but it is difficult for them to be objective when they could gain from your decision to invest in their products. Look for a qualified CPA, attorney, businessman, or banker who could give recommendations about a good planner. In general, try to find somebody who works on an hourly fee basis, who is willing to show his or her credentials, who will provide references, and whose income is provided primarily from planning—not from investing a client's money.[5]

How Much Are You Worth?

If you ever have applied for a loan or a line of credit, you probably filled out a statement of your net worth: what you own minus what you owe. The simplified financial planning questionnaire at the end of this chapter lets you update your assets and liabilities.

That questionnaire also asks about your financial goals. Have you thought about these? Caught in the pressures of working, paying bills, and trying to keep out of debt, sometimes we give no thought to future planning. That isn't good life management.

In pondering your financial goals, try to:

1. Think what major expenses you might have in the future—like education for your children, or retirement.

2. Evaluate whether you have sufficient disability, health, or life insurance.

3. Consider what you really need and want in the future. Both now and later, avoid purchasing things you can't use, don't need, or want only for status.

Even if your goals are modest and your net worth is small, consider having a will drawn up. That can save survivors a lot of hassle later.

Good Time Management Involves Control of Time Stealers

A cartoon shows a harried businessman reaching for a phone across a desk piled high with papers. "Sorry I can't talk about it now," the cartoon character says. "I'm late for my seminar on time management for successful leaders."

Do you ever feel like that businessman—so pressured with things to do that you can't even take time to think about time management? Each of us has the same 168 hours in a week, but we manage this time in different ways.

To some extent, this is because people see time differently. In some countries there is no rushing, people rarely think about punctuality, nobody pays much attention to clocks, and hardly anybody worries about time. We, in contrast, are much more controlled by the clock, but even in our culture people view time differently.[6]

• *Time as Your Master.* Some people feel controlled by time schedules and always have their eyes on their watches. These individuals avoid spontaneity, talk about "sneaking a break," or not being able to do something because "time won't allow it." Time is their master.

• *Time as Your Enemy.* Other people try to beat the clock, save time, or compete with past records. These people feel triumphant about being early or getting a lot done in a limited time period. They feel defeated when they arrive late or waste time.

• *Time as Your Slave.* This is the attitude of perpetually trying to make time count, to get control of time, and to not let time get away. People with this viewpoint want to be in charge of every minute. Maybe they see seconds as nuggets of gold that mustn't be lost or wasted.

• *Time as a Neutral Force.* Isn't this what time really is—twenty-four hours every day that can be wasted, used, controlled, or ignored? Time shouldn't be controlling me. I should be able to handle time with a minimum of worry, hassle, and frustration.

The Time Stealers

Often, time isn't managed well because it is stolen—by other people, by circumstances, and by our own attitudes. Think of the following ten time stealers as a checklist. How many apply to you? Notice that each is followed by suggestions for keeping time under your control.

• Time Stealer #1—*The tyranny of the urgent.* When he was a busy college president, Charles Hummel wrote a pamphlet suggesting that many time-management problems come about because we let urgent things crowd out important things.[7] How often have you started a day with projects to be done, but ended in frustration because your time was stolen by emergencies that grabbed your attention and pushed aside your careful plans?

Emergencies and urgent issues cannot be predicted and often they can't be ignored. But all is not hopeless. To control the tyranny of the urgent, find time for planning. Some time-management experts tell us to set aside one full day each month and a half day each week for planning. For some of us that isn't very realistic, but it is possible to take a few minutes at the end of each day to plan the next.

List what needs to be done. Make an estimate of the time needed for each activity. Then rank the items in order of importance. Roughly determine when, during the day, each item will be tackled. Keep enough flexibility in the planning to account for unexpected interruptions. If they occur, you have space in the schedule to deal with them. If they don't occur you have the pleasant experience of unexpected freedom to work on lower-priority items. Periodically, plan ahead in terms of the next week, the next month, and the next year.

When something "urgent" interrupts your time, ask yourself if it can wait. Phone calls need not always be taken immediately. Some so-called emergencies can wait.

All of us can get worried and inefficient if we constantly are overwhelmed by what needs to be done. Realistic planning lets you feel less pressured, even when emergencies arise. You might be encouraged by a former president of DuPont who said, "One minute spent in planning saves three or four minutes in execution."

• Time Stealer #2—*Interruptions.* Frequently, time is stolen, not by emergencies, but by routine disruptions that need not be handled immediately. If you work in an office and leave your door open, you are inviting people to "stick their heads in" whenever they pass. The mail does not need to be opened when it arrives. The telephone may not need to be answered whenever it rings. Calls don't need to be returned as soon as you get the message. Trips to the store need not be made as soon as you notice supplies are getting low.

It is better to make a note of these issues and set them aside to do later. If you are involved in one project and think of another, put the second project on a "to do" list and schedule time for it later. If you don't control the interruptions (including interruptions that come from your own thinking) they control you—and steal your time.

• Time Stealer #3—*Inefficiency.* It may take some experimenting, but most of us learn when we work most efficiently. I have discovered, for example, that I write best in the morning; I'm not as effective after lunch. Because of this I schedule writing times early and do more routine activities in the early afternoons.

Think about your own best work patterns. If possible, get the hardest and most unpleasant things out of the way as soon in the day as possible. Try to group activities so you handle all mail or all phone calls at once, rather than stringing different activities throughout the day.

• Time Stealer #4—*Lack of awareness.* Some people never think about time management. As a result, they lose a lot of time because of ignorance of their own inefficiency.

Keeping the records that we suggested earlier can help you see where time is going. It may be helpful to use gimmicks to improve awareness and help with your time management. When I was in graduate school, I counted the hours spent in the library. I deducted the time spent dozing or daydreaming and recorded my totals on a chart. Whenever I had an efficient day, I rewarded myself in some way. This motivated me to make better use of my time—and probably helped my grades.

• Time Stealer #5—*A defeatist attitude.* Do you ever feel like giving up in your attempts to manage time? Tell yourself, "There just isn't time," "I'll never have the time to do that," "It sure would be nice to have the time to . . ." and you are convincing yourself that time really can't be managed.

Try, instead, to challenge your own thinking. Tell yourself, "There *is* time to do what I really want." "I'll find the time to do. . . ." "Sure there will be time to complete this new project." This is taking a more positive attitude; accepting responsibility for your time and activities.

There is a danger in this, however. Some people are so

optimistic and positive about their future time that they get overcommitted and overwhelmed. They take on too much and constantly experience frustration because they can't get things done. Here, then, is another reason for prior planning. Some things that eat up time are beyond your control, but there are many other time-consuming activities that you can control. A lot depends on planning and your attitude.

• Time Stealer #6—*Disorganization.* You can lose time when you can't find a book, telephone number, or file. It takes time to get organized, but when things are kept in order, you can get what you need quickly and with less time loss.

• Time Stealer #7—*Immobilization.* Do you ever look at a big project and feel so overwhelmed that you do nothing, except waste time thinking about getting started? An alternative is to divide and conquer. Break down the big projects into smaller tasks that can be managed. Remember the old story about the journey of a thousand miles that is made one step at a time. It starts with the first step.

• Time Stealer #8—*Overwork and other bad habits.* In our society, we admire hard work and reward diligent activity. Overwork can wear us down, however, and tired people waste time because they are less efficient.

As we will see in the next chapter, efficiency is reduced by improper diet, lack of exercise, insufficient rest, overuse of alcohol or tobacco, avoidance of vacations, and a workaholic attitude that wears out the body. We waste time when we don't take care of ourselves.

Take time to relax, and you are more likely to make better use of time when you work. If long breaks are impossible, try mini-vacations—taking off an afternoon, taking time for a nap, reading a few pages of some relaxing book, getting away briefly from demanding people, spending time with a hobby. All of this is good time management.

• Time Stealer #9—*The one-man show.* Nobody does a

job like we do it ourselves. Regrettably, some people try to do everything themselves and waste a lot of time as a result.

Management has been defined as the art of getting things done by other people. Ask yourself if others could be doing what you do. Can you delegate some responsibilities? How could you get help? Who could do a capable job of handling some of your responsibilities? It takes a while to train others, to supervise, to give praise, but in the long run this saves time for you. Even if you aren't a manager, think how others could help you save time.

• Time Stealer #10—*Saying yes too often and too quickly.* You've had the experience. An opportunity is presented that will take time in the future. You can see its value, think highly of the person who is asking, and don't want to hurt or disappoint others. So you say yes without careful thinking. Later you regret your decision because your schedule is overcommitted. And the overcommitment is your own fault.

Try to think before you say yes. Ask if you really will have time to do what is being asked. Will it help people, help your career, keep you from doing something else of importance, create extra pressure on you and your family, run counter to your goals? If you must say no, try to be gracious. Express thanks for the invitation, explain your reasons for saying no, and politely refuse to be pressured or manipulated. You may feel uncomfortable now but you'll thank yourself later.

Giving Is Fulfilling

The Rotterdam newspaper recently carried a story that surprised a lot of readers. Piet Derksen, a Dutch millionaire and one of Holland's richest men, announced that he was planning to turn his private company into a publicly held corporation and donate $150 million in proceeds to charitable projects in the Third World. Sole owner of a European sports equipment company with 1,600 employees, the seventy-one-year-old Mr. Derksen decided to sell his two thousand shares on the stock exchange and give the proceeds to projects that help the sick and poor. His art collection, worth an estimated $650,000, was part of the deal. It was to be auctioned off, with the money going to charity.

The newspaper article didn't say how the gentleman's children or business colleagues reacted to this decision. But Mr. Derksen was outspoken.

"My wealth has been like a stone around my neck," he said. "I'm glad to get rid of it. I could shout for joy."

Most people, I suspect, are more inclined to shout for joy when they accumulate riches. The more we get, the more we want; and the more we get, the less we are inclined to pass it on to others.

Mr. Derksen may have discovered an important principle of resource management, however: There is joy and fulfillment in giving. I know of no research to support this conclusion, but many have experienced the liberation that this Dutch businessman felt when he was willing to give.

Jesus said that it is more blessed to give than to receive (Acts 20:35). The members of Alcoholics Anonymous demonstrate this every day when they give their time, energies, and money to help one another. Is it possible that people with a giving attitude are less uptight, more relaxed, and more inclined to be mentally healthy?

None of this undercuts the importance of good money and time management. Nevertheless, good life management recognizes that fulfillment comes not only in controlling what we possess, but in sharing what we can give.

There can be no better illustration than Louisa May Alcott, the famous author, who chose to manage her life by giving to others.

Financial Planning Questionnaire

1. What are your assets and liabilities? Complete the following chart. Use more paper if needed.

    Assets (What You Own)

Savings	$_____
Checking account	_____
Value of car	_____
Value of house	_____
Resale value of furniture and possessions	_____
Cash value of insurance	_____
Other	_____
	_____
Total	_____

    Liabilities (What You Owe)

Unpaid car balance	_____
Mortgage	_____
Personal loans	_____
	_____
Credit cards and other debts	_____
	_____
	_____
Total	_____

    Net Worth (Difference Between Assets and Liabilities) _____

Date: _____

2. Make a list of your financial goals. Use two columns. In one column write the things you need. In the other column write what you want.

3. Look over your two lists and put numbers next to each item. Put a 1 next to things you plan to attain as soon as possible, a 2 for things that can wait a while, a 3 for things that are of lowest priority.

4. What is the next step you will take in attaining your number 1 goals? Be specific.

Nine

Managing
Your
Self

The first call came to police headquarters at 2:50 in the morning. Three local residents on their way to the airport had spotted a lion stalking through the quiet, darkened neighborhoods of Waukegan.

A police car went to investigate but all was serene.

Then came another telephone call. And another. The lion had been seen again, racing across a park—its sleek body sliding through the predawn mist, its mane flowing in the breeze, its long tail with the fluffy crop of fur on the end leaving no doubt that this was indeed a lion on the loose.

These reports were taken more seriously. Ten police and animal-control officers sped to the scene of the sightings. The radio alerted early risers to be careful. Somebody called the zoo to see if any lions were missing. Were there any circuses in the area? The big lion search was on.

Meanwhile, Henny had gone home and was sleeping

peacefully. He should have been on duty all night, guarding the local wrecking company, but the ninety-pound German shepherd had found a hole in the fence. Before going to sleep he had gone for a run. How could Henny know he looked like a lion?

Several days earlier, Henny's owner had taken the dog to get a summer haircut. "I wanted him to be cool," the owner said, "and we thought it might be fun to have Henny shaved to look like a lion. People do this to poodles and cocker spaniels, so we decided to give Henny a new look."

When Henny's nocturnal escapades were discovered, his owner wondered if there would be criminal charges against him. But nobody could find a local ordinance prohibiting German shepherds from impersonating lions.

So the wrecking company fixed the hole in the fence, and Henny had his picture in all the local papers.

In the Eye of the Beholder

Why would anybody mistake a German shepherd for a lion? Henny's unusual haircut made him look like the king of beasts, especially during the night when it was dark. Any of us could have made the same mistake. The locals laughed the next day when they realized how many had been fooled by the "lion of Waukegan."

Beauty, we have all heard, is in the eye of the beholder. When you're in love you may see beauty that nobody else can see. When you think there's danger in your community, you may hear threatening sounds that nobody else hears. When you are seriously ill but hoping to recover, you may notice signs of improvement that the doctor doesn't see. A lot of life—how we think and act—depends on how we see the world. And a lot of life management depends on our perceptions of others, of circumstances, of ourselves.

How do you see others? From your perspective, is the

world a friendly place or is it a jungle filled with human lions, intent on devouring one another? How do you perceive your family members, your work colleagues, your neighbors, your boss? Our views of others, and their views of us, may be partially inaccurate, but we all act as if our perceptions are true. Your behavior depends largely on what you see.

How do you see your circumstances? Is your neighborhood safe, your job secure, your life fulfilling? Can things be changed and improved or do you feel trapped by circumstances that seem beyond your control?

How do you see yourself? If you were writing a character sketch of yourself, what would you include? Think about it for a minute. You might even want to write out a list of your qualities. Are you friendly, competent, humorous, insecure, filled with feelings of inferiority, rigid, sensitive, intolerant, kind? Other people may see you differently, but you likely will act in accordance with the way you see yourself.

This had led some counselors and life-management experts to conclude that changing a person's perceptions, including self-perceptions, is the best way to change behavior. When the people in Waukegan realized that their "lion" was really a friendly German shepherd, they relaxed because their perceptions had changed. Their anxiety turned to amusement.

To change yourself and to manage life more effectively, you may need to change some of your viewpoints. Start by getting to know yourself better. Then you can decide what needs to be changed, and how this can be done.

Self-Management Involves Self-Knowledge

Many years ago an energetic young man went to work in a neighborhood hardware store. The business had been around for years and the shelves and bins included thousands of dollars worth of items that were obsolete, collecting dust, and unlikely to ever sell.

It took time, but the new employee eventually convinced the store owner to set up a table in the middle of an aisle where the old items could be sold. Each was priced at ten cents.

So successful was the sale that the young man got permission to hold another. One day he got the idea of opening an entire store that would sell only nickel and dime items. He volunteered to be the manager if his boss would supply the capital.

The employer was not enthusiastic. He was sure the plan would never work because nobody could find enough nickel and dime items to fill a whole store.

You can guess what happened. The disappointed young employee quit his job at the hardware store and went ahead with his plan. He even named his stores after himself, F. W. Woolworth.

Years later the old boss lamented, "As far as I can tell, every word I used to turn Woolworth down has cost me about a million dollars!"

F. W. Woolworth must have known some of his own strengths. Early in life he became aware of his own business sense. He must have known that people with accurate knowledge of the business world are best able to manage their companies. In the same way, people with accurate knowledge of their own inner worlds are best able to manage their lives.

There are at least three ways to increase your self-knowledge.

Reflecting on Your Self

Most psychological tests are designed to give information about the test taker—his or her abilities, aptitudes, interests, intellectual capabilities, personality traits, values, and strengths. Tests are helpful because they give objective perspectives and often compare the test taker with others of the same age and educational level.

Even without tests, you can discover a lot by yourself— sitting back in a chair and thinking about your characteristics, weaknesses, and areas of strength.

Many people (me included) also find it helpful to keep a journal for recording daily happenings and observations about life. This need not be something fancy. It can be an inexpensive notebook, purchased at the modern equivalent of those old F. W. Woolworth stores.

A journal "is a tool for self discovery," writes Ronald Klug in his book on journal keeping.[1] Your journal could be an aid to concentration, "a place to generate and capture ideas, a safety valve for the emotions, a training ground for the writer, and a good friend and confidant." Its value is so powerful that a well-known psychologist, Dr. Ira Progoff, has built both a professional reputation and an entire system of therapy around the keeping of an "intensive journal."[2]

Writing, says novelist R. V. Cassill, is "a way of coming to terms with the world and with oneself."[3] It can be a beautiful and rewarding experience for discovering one's self.[4] It is an aid to concentration, a help in thinking about the present or planning for the future, a place to reflect on one's values and spiritual beliefs, a means for thinking about strengths and weaknesses, a record of significant events, and a place to work out frustrations, hostilities, attitudes, hurts, and misunderstandings.

How do you keep a journal? There are no rules, no demands for proper grammar, no requirements to say how often you write or how long to make each entry. I write when I feel like it. That may be every few days, or several times in one day. What I write varies in length and the subject matter is diverse.

Try to be honest when you write. Record daily happenings, your feelings, your plans for the future, your struggles, the things you learn from your reading and interactions with others. For variety, sometime try writing about yourself in the third person. Describe yourself as seen by your mother, your closest friend, your employer, or some critic. Express your feelings in a letter that you never will mail. Try writing a letter to God. Make a list of your gifts and abilities. Take your journal on vacation to record your experiences. Occasionally insert a photograph or newspaper clipping. Jot down quotations from others that are worth remembering.

Many have found journal writing to be a powerful aid to self-discovery. The only way to know if it helps you is to try it. The cost amounts to almost nothing.

Revealing Your Self

Sidney Jourard was a psychologist who believed in self-disclosure. "No man can come to know himself except as an outcome of disclosing himself to another person," Jourard wrote in *The Transparent Self.*[5] People who are willing to make themselves known to at least one other significant human being are people who get along better with others, handle stress more effectively, and are less inclined to withdraw into various forms of mental illness.

Self-disclosure takes courage, and sometimes it can be overdone. Nevertheless, the Delphi oracle's advice to "know thyself" still has merit, and Jourard's paraphrase is worth pondering carefully: *Make thyself known, and thou shalt then know thyself.*[6]

Reading to Understand Your Self

Self-help books sometimes get criticized, even by writers of other self-help books. Often the criticisms are justified.

There are many books written by poorly qualified people who offer simplistic and sometimes harmful advice.

Not all books fall into that category. Many are written by competent authors who have done their homework and who write with care, clarity, accuracy, and a strong desire to be practical. Before you read a book, check the writer's credentials. Do you know anyone who would recommend the book? If you decide to read it, keep thinking as you go through the pages. Ideas and conclusions are not always correct, just because they are in print. Authors, like everybody else, can be wrong.

If you want to read to understand yourself, try not to stick with self-help books, useful as these may be. Read the Bible, great literature from the past, well-written fiction, and general articles that increase your understanding and accurate perceptions of the world in which we live. The most interesting people on this planet are those who continually expand their horizons through reading and exposure to new insights and information.

Self-Management Involves Control of Your Body

The health club advertisements say it all:

You can build a better body.

You can take off weight, shape up, and have more sex appeal.

You can be more beautiful—in just ninety days.

"Imagine getting the body you've dreamed of," one brochure exclaims. If you're a man, the body builder promises to "give you bulges as big as you want them, where you want them." Women are promised help to "get rid of bulges where you don't want them."

The recent American fascination with fitness is probably good. Some would credit the baby-boom generation for re-

minding all of us that we can't have well-managed lives if
we are careless about managing our bodies.

Mind and Body

Would you agree with the ethics professor who thinks
"we live in an age of unprecedented adoration of, and attack
on, the human body"?[7] We do appear to have different attitudes about our bodies; attitudes that form in the mind and
determine how we take care of ourselves. We will consider
several of these.

Meaningless bodies—the body ignored. Until they start
acting up or stop running smoothly, many of us take our
bodies for granted. We aren't careful what we feed them.
We allow them no rest, fill them with drugs or alcohol, and
never give them exercise. Such a mind-set assumes the
body is meaningless and not worth considering in terms of
our life plans.

Can people who ignore or pay little attention to their
bodies really be good life managers? What does it profit individuals if they manage whole corporations with careful
attention to detail, but let their own bodies run down
through neglect?

Mistreated bodies—the body pushed. Sometimes we
push our bodies to the breaking point—and then we are
surprised when they collapse.

Probably you have seen some of the health-tip brochures
distributed by local hospitals or physicians. Recently we received a pamphlet describing ways to fight cancer.[8] Most of
the suggestions were obvious but they pointed to things we
often forget.

Eat wisely, said the brochure. A balanced, nutritious diet
may be the best defense against cancer and most other diseases. Include fresh vegetables, fruits, whole-grain cereals
and breads. Drink several glasses of water every day. Re-

duce your consumption of fried foods and try to avoid eating things that are high in sugar, salt, and fat. The fat we eat and the fat we wear can both be dangerous. Poorly fed bodies are mistreated bodies.

Then, says the hospital brochure, we should reduce or eliminate alcohol consumption, cut the intake of coffee, and stop smoking. According to careful research findings, 30 percent of all cancer deaths are related to cigarette smoking.

Excessive exposure to sunlight can be a villain too. Every year, four hundred thousand Americans are affected by skin cancer. In an estimated 90 percent of the cases, the cancer comes at least in part because of excessive exposure to the sun's ultraviolet rays.

Have regular checkups, advises the brochure writer. The older we get, the more this is important.

To neglect these basic health-care principles is to mistreat the body, to put it under pressure, and to slow down its efficient functioning.

Meritless bodies—the body destroyed. Nimrod was the Babylonian god of war. His goal was to destroy whole nations, to injure, and to kill.

Sometimes we treat bodies, especially other people's bodies, as if they can be sacrificed and exploited. War does this. The slave trade did this and so do modern acts of racism, family abuse, sexual exploitation, violence, and terrorism. The employer who pushes workers to their limits, and beyond, is demonstrating a selfish disregard for the bodies of others.

Sometimes the disregard starts with ourselves. Drug abuse, gluttony, uncontrolled drinking, unbridled lust— these can destroy our own bodies and create havoc in our families and businesses.

Mastered bodies—the body performing. Somebody has suggested that we worship the god of athleticism. We heap acclaim and dollars on professional athletes and admire those who can discipline their bodies to perform feats of endurance and skill.

Surely you have heard the suggestion that professional football involves a few muscular men, desperately in need of rest, performing for thousands of observers, desperately in need of exercise. It is fine to admire the bodies and physical capabilities of others, but sitting and watching does nothing to get people like you and me into better physical shape.

Me-centered bodies—the body admired. Do you remember the story of Narcissus? He was a figure in Greek mythology who greatly admired and gazed at his own body. In an era when there were no mirrors, Narcissus looked frequently at his own reflection in a pool. One day he lost his balance and drowned in the water, but his name still lives whenever we describe someone who is narcissistic.

Business managers are encouraged to dress for success and pay attention to personal appearance. Narcissistic people go further. They can be obsessed with personal grooming, body building, physical fitness, perfect figures, and high fashion. In themselves, none of these is bad, but pursuit of the body beautiful can be harmful. It distracts us from other activities, can make us insensitive to other people, and lets self-centered narcissism interfere with other areas of effective life management.

"Build a better body with the right equipment," says a magazine advertisement, graced with the picture of a slim, attractive female and a muscular, good-looking male. Readers are encouraged to spend money buying gimmicks that are guaranteed to produce magnificent bodies. This, says one observer, is evidence of the cult of bodily perfection: Humans seeking to have bodies like Narcissus and the ancient Greek gods.[9]

For most of us that isn't going to happen.

Sweet Talk

Still, we can take care of our bodies, realizing that this can greatly affect the way we manage the rest of our lives.

As one example, consider refined sugar. Candy, pastries, desserts, and soda pops are not the only foods that contain sugar. There is more sugar in one hamburger bun than in a four-ounce piece of cheesecake. Half a cup of orange juice has the same amount of sugar as a cream puff. A serving of sherbet has over three times more sugar than an equal size serving of ice cream.[10]

Is this important? Sugar gives quick energy, but it can leave us feeling weak, tired, depressed, and craving harmful foods, including more sugar. Too much sugar in the system slows us down and hinders clear-thinking life management. Similar charges could be leveled against caffeine, white flour, high-salt products (including many snack foods), fatty meats, and most fried fast-foods.

Information like this can be discouraging. It seems that no matter what you eat, your body will be harmed in some way. Do you ever feel like giving up on careful eating because it seems the only way to keep from poisoning your body is to stop eating altogether?

A better goal is to strive for a balanced diet, to avoid the obvious culprits (fats, salts, and sugars), and to eat everything else in moderation. This can improve your physical fitness and give the clearer thinking that lets you manage the rest of your life more effectively.

Self-Management Involves Keeping in Shape

In his many years of public polling, George Gallup called it "one of the most dramatic changes in life-style" he had

seen. In the early 1960s only 24 percent of adults in the
United States exercised regularly. Fifteen years later the
number had almost doubled, and it seems to have been increasing ever since.[11]

Stress and fitness expert Kenneth Pelletier can see no
simple explanation to account for this trend that involves
nearly 100 million people. Almost overnight, "millions of
men and women have given up smoking, are exercising and
jogging, are eating healthier diets, have lost weight, are
managing stress more effectively, and are moving toward
optimum health and longevity."[12]

Sometimes this physical activity leaves something to be
desired. One lady decided to take up jogging after listening
to a television interview that described the dangers of inactivity. She began in the middle of winter and wrote her observations following the fourth day:

> Where is the *high* I'm supposed to achieve? I just returned
> from my fourth day of jogging and I'm at an all-time low. If I
> could catch my breath I would sob. As it is, the tears are
> frozen to my face and I feel like I don't have long to live. The
> calves of my legs are having labor pains and I *know* what
> they will give birth to—charley horses! Are ladies really
> supposed to sweat this way?
> By the way . . . , where do you get those cute little running
> suits for less than the price of a VW Rabbit?[13]

The lady persisted with what she called a program of
"wogging"—a combination of both walking and jogging.
Within a few months she felt healthier, less inclined to lose
her breath, more efficient in her work. Exercise, she found,
"is more than a beauty aid. It strengthens the heart muscle,
helps circulation, keeps other muscles working, keeps com-
plexions clear and healthy, and gives you a good feeling
about yourself."[14]

Such exercise is best done in moderation. Strenuous
physical activity can be hazardous to your health and the

experts in physical fitness urge people to use restraint in their fitness programs. "Jogging has lost its chic," says one news report. "Walking and bicycling are in. Overdoing it is out; doing nothing at all is out too." The new fitness motto is Walk, don't run.[15] Presumably wogging is okay!

Even if you hate wogging or any other kind of formal exercise and have no interest in sports, you still can work on physical fitness in more natural ways. Walk for twenty minutes a day in loose-fitting clothes and soft shoes. Take stairs instead of elevators. Don't park so near the shopping center door, park farther out and walk. Forget the golf cart and walk around the course. Carry your bags into the airport instead of giving them to a porter. Walk behind the lawn mower instead of riding all the time. Dr. Norbert M. Sander, Jr., founder of the Preventive and Sports Medical Center in New York, calls this the "M & M" approach to physical fitness: *moving more.*

Fighting Fatigue

It also helps if you rest more.

Have you ever noticed how your efficiency slips when you get tired? Pressured by deadlines and impressed with the importance of achievements, many of us keep pushing when we should be resting. Soon we see productivity go down. It takes longer to accomplish even simple tasks. If the fatigue builds over time, we are much more likely to get depressed. Irritability, insensitivity, and increased numbers of mistakes all follow in the wake of fatigue.

Do you get enough rest? How much we need varies from person to person, of course, but the American Medical Association recommends seven to eight hours sleep per night. People who regularly sleep more than nine hours or less than six have a higher risk of fatal heart disease, cancer, or stroke.[16]

Have you ever worked for weeks or even months on some intense, high-energy project and noticed no decline in efficiency or energy— until the project ends? The body can rally for a long period of time but at the end there needs to be time for rejuvenation and making up for lost rest.

There have been times in my life when I have tried to do two projects, one immediately after the other, and have paid a price physically because I didn't allow for rest time in between. I can't run off on a speaking trip for two or three weeks and expect to resume teaching or writing on the first day back. There has to be "turn around time" that includes sufficient time for rest and relaxation. Physiologists have discovered that the body needs to rejuvenate and make some chemical readjustments after we have extended ourselves on a project. Sometimes the chemical readjustments are accompanied by temporary fatigue and depression. To ignore this is to fight your own body and slow its recovery. Getting rest is a good principle for life management.

By reflecting on your life experiences have you reached any personal conclusions about self-management? The informal questionnaire at the end of this chapter may help as you think about your own life.

Self-Management Involves Self-Control

Periodically, I travel to military bases where I give workshops, often on life-management topics. Recently my travels took me to a remote Mediterranean air base where service personnel are assigned for fifteen-month periods away from their homes and families. Before my arrival, I received a letter from the chaplain telling me what to expect.

"The people here are bored and lonely," he wrote. Even though they were working long hours, many had difficulty controlling their drinking, discouragement, and sexual urges. Prostitution, homosexuality, and drug use were more prevalent than anyone wanted to admit. Efficiency in some people was declining because of a lack of self-control.

This is an old problem and one that is faced far beyond the confines of a military base. How do we control stubborn habits? Why do we give in to urges and temptations that we really want to resist?

Near the end of the sixth century, the first archbishop of Canterbury wrote about his years of struggle with a sexual compulsion. "When desire is given satisfaction, habit is forged and when habit passes unresisted a compulsive urge sets in." This description by Saint Augustine sounds ancient and stuffy, but it is surprisingly accurate in describing how individuals lose self-control.[17]

First, you give in once to some behavior and enjoy the experience. Augustine would say yielding to desire gives satisfaction; psychologists would say your behavior has been reinforced.

So you give in again. This is followed by more satisfaction. There may be a little guilt, but this passes and soon you yield again—and again. Before long, you have developed a habit. Some habits, like sexual activities, give pleasure. Others, like drinking, may help people avoid feelings of discouragement or distress. In both cases the habit continues because it is satisfying.

When the habit is repeated consistently, it can become a compulsion that seems impossible to stop. The compulsive drinker, for example, may first become psychologically addicted to alcohol, but then the body becomes physically addicted. The quickest way to get rid of the uncomfortable psychological and bodily symptoms is to drink more.

Self-Watching

Is there any way to break out of this cycle? When physical addictions have developed, you need medical treatment to help the body readjust. Fortunately, most self-control problems don't have that physical involvement so self-control may be easier.

Try to think of self-control as a long-term, four-step process that begins with self-watching.

What is a habit or behavior you want to eliminate? For the next week or two, carry a little notebook and keep a record of every time you are tempted to give in. You might call this your self-watching diary.[18] Write down:

1. The date and time when you were tempted to yield.
2. The place and situation. Were you in a tense situation? Were you in a store? Were you looking at magazines? Were you passing a bakery or a bar?
3. Who you were with—friends, family, your boss, yourself, others.
4. Your feelings at the time. Were you angry, bored, tense, discouraged, lonely?
5. Your thoughts. What were you saying to yourself at the time of the temptation? What was going through your mind?
6. The outcome. Did you give in to the urge or did you resist?

Do you know what makes you drink, gamble, overwork, lose your temper, or eat too much? Maybe you've thought, *If only I knew, then I could control myself.* One way to know is to watch yourself for a while.

Self-Management

It seems obvious, perhaps, but the next step to self-control is to look over your self-watch diary. What are the cues that trigger undesirable acts in you? Can you take deliberate steps to avoid tempting circumstances?

When I'm trying to watch my weight (that's most of the time), I avoid Sunday brunches and buffet restaurants where it is easy to pile a plate high with all kinds of delicious and tempting gourmet delicacies. It is less tempting, and easier to control my eating, when we go to sit-down restaurants that deemphasize desserts. It also helps if we keep the house free of ice cream, cookies, bread and rolls, snack foods, and similar temptations.

This is a simple rule, but often forgotten: If you want to control temptations, stay away from the places, situations, people, and objects that are likely to tempt you. Maybe you will need to rearrange your schedule, leisure time activities, shopping habits, or the places you go on vacation.

Self-Talk

Regrettably, it isn't always possible to rearrange our lives and avoid tempting situations. Here is where self-talk can be helpful. When you can't or haven't avoided a tempting situation try to:

• *Pause before responding.* Tell yourself to wait ten minutes. Often the cravings will go away during that time, you will slow down to think more rationally, and you will have time to think ahead to consider the long-term consequences of giving in.

• *Challenge your own thinking.* You could tell yourself, "I just don't have the willpower to stop overeating," but that simply isn't true. Instead tell yourself, "There's no such thing as willpower, just poor planning. If I use self-watching techniques, even *I* can change my eating habits."

• *Use your imagination.* Think of yourself as looking slim, being successful, or uncontrolled by impulses. Think of yourself talking calmly with someone who makes you angry and imagine that you each are showing respect and self-restraint. In an earlier chapter we quoted Denis Waitley, who wrote: "Life is a self-prophecy; you won't necessarily get what you want in life, but in the long run you will usually get what you expect."[19] This applies to self-control just as it applies to the rest of life.

Some people use their imaginations to picture themselves in less stressful or less tempting situations. When tension makes you inclined to explode, temporarily imagine yourself in a quiet place, free from noise and pressure from others. This sometimes is labeled visualization; others call it fantasy. In limited amounts and for short periods of time, these mental exercises can help with self-control.

Self-Direction

Self-control is more likely to persist if you direct your own behavior. Try to:

- Reward yourself when you do succeed in self-control.
- Constantly be alert to tempting situations—some self-watching will always be necessary.
- Plan ahead so you can avoid temptations—if you are tempted to drink too much at the company party, plan, before you go, how this can be avoided.
- Get a little help from your friends—often we can help each other at self-control.
- Plan enjoyable alternatives that give pleasure in place of the temptations you are trying to avoid.
- Practice analyzing and changing negative thinking that leads to discouragement, anger, anxiety, and self-criticism.

If self-control still remains a problem, you may want to talk to a counselor. Sometimes there are deeper reasons for your compulsive behavior—reasons that a counselor could help you uncover. Some people really don't want to change. Others have discovered, unconsciously perhaps, that their habits are powerful weapons for annoying family members. The frustrated husband who keeps drinking to get his wife angry, or the bright student who consistently aggravates her parents by getting poor grades *may* be involved in psychological issues that don't always yield to our four guidelines for self-control.

Self-Management Involves Handling Change

Jack Levering recently published a book. It isn't very long and the sales haven't been good—seventy-two copies thus far—but the author really doesn't care. Now in his late sixties, living alone, he doesn't have a lot to do. But he always wanted to write a book.

So he did.

"I wrote it for me," he said in a newspaper interview. "I'm not sure it's something the general public would enjoy. It has no sex, no violence, no murder, and no filth."

It was of no interest to the big New York publishers, so Jack Levering found a press that would print it for a price. He took $11,000 from his savings and mailed the check along with his manuscript of anecdotes, poems, letters, stories from his past, and personal memorabilia. "It's who I am," he said, when the copies arrived. "It's not any world-shaking thing. It's me. It's my soul. It's my song."[20]

Like all of us, Jack Levering lives in a changing world. When he retired, he adapted to the changes by turning to his book, doing something he had always wanted to do—even though some people thought he was foolish.

Mastering Change

Change is natural, writes Leon Martel of the Hudson Institute. Changes occur constantly and to get our lives out of
neutral we must learn to adapt.

A specialist in mastering change,[21] Martel notes that
many people plan for the future by looking back to see
what has happened in the past. "Look at the number of
business plans and forecasts that begin—'If present trends
continue. . . .' But the truth is that present trends often *don't*
continue, or they may fluctuate in size, direction, or rate of
development."[22]

Change, however, isn't all random. Many changes are ir-
reversible, ongoing, and predictable. We are all getting
older, prices are increasing, the society is becoming less of
an industrial economy and more of an information-sharing
culture. Corporations and individuals should look around,
see what is happening, and make long-term plans. Some
people deny change, rarely think ahead, and wonder why
they are surprised when predictable changes occur.

Whenever you encounter change, whether it comes as a
surprise or was predictable, try to:

1. Pause long enough to get a perspective on the situation. Others can often help. Is the situation really as bad or
as threatening as it seems? Could there be benefits to the
change? Look on the positive side.

2. Think of actions you could take to cope with change.
Write your solutions on paper. What is and is not realistic?
What will you do first?

3. Consider the ways you handled change in the past.
What was helpful and what was not? What can you learn
from your past successes and failures?

4. Admit that some people handle change better than
others. Some thrive on it, others do not. Remember that no
person needs to be immobilized by change. Face it, think
what to do about it, and take action.

5. Decide if there are some changes you plan to ignore. My parents are retired. They continue to keep up-to-date in many things, but neither plans to learn how to run a computer. This is a deliberate decision that makes sense for them. There may be similar areas in all our lives where we decide to let change pass us by.

Good life managers don't use this as an excuse to do nothing. We keep abreast of the areas that are most important and work to manage our lives successfully, even in an exciting world that is changing so fast most of us have difficulty keeping up.

Maybe I . . . Should Make Some Changes

The following is a fill-in-the-blanks exercise designed to help you think about your own life management.

Answer the following questions by writing something that is true in your life right now. Don't ponder your answers too long. Write what tends to come to mind on first thought.

Maybe I . . .

1. could manage life better if I_____

_____

2. don't need to_____
3. still ought to_____
4. should accept the fact that_____

_____

5. would be in better physical shape if I_____

_____

6. moved too quickly when I_____
7. would get along better if I_____

_____

8. shouldn't_____
9. should_____

_____ once again

10. need to_____

_____ sometime soon

11. should try_____
12. am now ready to _____
13. will have a better future if I_____

_____

Are you surprised at what you wrote in the blanks? Do your answers suggest some guidelines for better life management? How could this help you change? Be specific.

Ten

Managing

Your

Destiny

Some might say his life didn't make any sense. He was a child of the previous century, eldest son in a family of nine children. His father, a rural midwestern minister, stretched a meager income to provide food and shelter, but there was nothing left for the niceties of life.

When he was old enough to work, Otto Keller left home to find employment in the rough-and-tumble construction industry. His honesty, reliability, and youthful energy led to repeated successes. People called him a "self-made man" when he was still in his twenties, living proof that hard work and determination do bring prosperity.

Imagine the surprise of his neighbors when the young Otto Keller abruptly disposed of his thriving business, turned away from his promising future, pulled together all his assets, and sailed for Africa. He went on his own, with no promise of a salary, no human agency or relief organization to back his decision, no knowledge of anyone who would meet him when he stepped off the boat in East Africa. None of this made much sense to the people he left in upper Michigan.

Why did he go?

The decision was spurred by the death of his closest friend, a young man who had gone to Africa to work as a lay missionary. When word drifted out of the African bush that the harsh, drought-ridden conditions had snuffed out the life of his friend, Otto Keller was deeply moved. With characteristic determination and dedication, he decided to take up the task of helping needy and suffering Africans. He would replace his friend.

While the ship inched along the hot, sultry coast of the great dark continent, World War I erupted in Europe. Hostilities quickly spread and soon British and German colonial forces were fighting fiercely in the sweltering African hinterlands. Travel for visitors was restricted, so Otto Keller offered his services to the British authorities in Kenya. They appointed him to serve in famine relief and sent him six hundred miles inland to a station near Lake Victoria.

It was there he would spend the rest of his life.

Many years later, Otto Keller's son described the work and dedication of his pioneer father:

> He was not blinded by self-conceit or personal pride. . . . Fame, recognition, human credentials were of little consequence. . . . Nor did he ever seek for the applause and plaudits of his contemporaries in the civilized world.
>
> Amid the surging masses of men and women with hands outstretched for a handful of cornmeal or a spoonful of beans, Dad became in truth a father to the fatherless, a friend to the forlorn, a tower of hope to those without hope. . . .
>
> The huts and villages built of mud and sticks, plastered with cow dung, were crude and filthy hovels in which human beings, goats, chickens, and a few scrub cattle lived together at a bestial level. With utter boldness and unflinch-

ing courage, Dad and Mother entered these places to bring help and healing. Their love and compassion was shed abroad so freely in their visits that many of the villagers were drawn from their despair to discover a new life in God.[1]

Few of Otto Keller's friends back in America ever knew of his dedication to the African people, his respect for their inherent intelligence, or his tireless efforts in teaching them how to till the soil, irrigate land, raise crops, build stable homes, and even beautify their surroundings with flowers. Few heard how the Kellers built schools and hospitals, improved nutrition, taught principles of hygiene, instructed the people in carpentry and farming skills, and willingly taught others how to be teachers of their own people. When he died at age fifty-four, Otto Keller left a legacy of schools staffed with qualified African teachers, several hundred churches pastored by trained Christian leaders, and uncounted thousands of new believers.

Even cynics agree that his life made an impact, but his son summarized Otto Keller's real motivation. He believed he "had an enormous job to do for God, and he got on with it. It was sufficient for him to please Christ and be a benefit to others around him."[2]

The Keller home was always open. No stranger was ever turned away even when supplies were limited. These remarkably dedicated people "simply trusted God their Father for every aspect of life. It was he who had brought them to this spot. He would keep them there. He would lead them on from here. All was well!"[3]

From a modern perspective, this kind of thinking makes little sense and it hardly serves as a good model for life management. But the Kellers didn't worry about that. They were sustained and motivated by their deep faith—a faith that gave their lives fulfillment and meaning.

Effective Life Management Is Easier When There Is Meaning in Life

Human beings are the only creatures who are known to think about their own destinies and reasons for existing. Why are we here? What is the purpose of life? To what extent do we determine our own life outcomes? What is there about living that gives fulfillment and meaning?

Questions like these delight philosophers, stump experts, and sometimes give the rest of us feelings of discomfort and anxiety. When sixty university students were asked why they had attempted suicide, 85 percent replied that "life seemed meaningless." Surprisingly, 93 percent of these suicide-attempters had active social lives, good grades, and positive relationships with their families. But their lives lacked meaning.[4]

In a survey of psychotherapists, the majority reported that many people enter psychotherapy because their lives lack meaning and a clear sense of purpose.[5] The crisis of meaninglessness is stated succinctly by I. D. Yalom: "How does a being who needs meaning find meaning in a universe that has no meaning?"[6] We need meaning to survive, Yalom concluded. When there is no meaning, there is no purpose in living.

And there is little reason for working on life management.

Many years ago, psychiatrist Viktor Frankl reached a similar conclusion. Months of imprisonment in the Nazi death camp at Auschwitz led to his theory of *logotherapy*, an approach to counseling that helps people find "healing through meaning." The search for meaning is a primary goal for all of us, Frankl concluded. His observations at Auschwitz showed that inmates handled stress better and had a greater chance to survive when they had clear beliefs or could see some purpose for living. People who have meaning in life can survive almost any kind of suffering.[7]

Where Do You Go to Find Meaning?

Otto Keller and his wife found meaning in their work with the people of Africa, but what about the rest of us? Where do we go to find meaning? According to several research studies, people with a positive sense of meaning in life

- are more stable than those without meaning—the less meaning in your life, the more likely you are to develop emotional and behavioral disturbances;
- tend to be interested in the welfare of others and are concerned about bettering humanity;
- are dedicated to some cause and have a clear sense of life goals;
- are flexible in their quests for meaning—as we grow older, many of us find meaning in new or different tasks and interests; and
- have a set of religious beliefs.[8]

Could there be any better description of Otto Keller? Could such a description apply to you?

Effective Life Managers Develop a Useful Philosophy of Life

A philosophy of life consists of those beliefs, attitudes, and values that guide our thinking and govern our actions.[9]

You may not have thought much about this, but probably you have accepted a group of assumptions and personal beliefs that direct your life. Do you think people can be

trusted? Do you believe God exists? Do you agree with the
psychoanalysist who wrote, "man is alone in a universe in-
different to his fate"? Do you agree with Shakespeare that
"life is a tale told by an idiot and signifying nothing"? Do
you share Otto Keller's belief that God is compassionate
and so interested in individual human beings that He wants
us to find fulfillment through faithful service to Him? Your
answers to questions like these can give a clue to your philosophy of life.

People find genuine life meaning in a number of places.
Many of us, for example, find authentic meaning and personal fulfillment come through work, family involvements,
creative activities or hobbies, participation in sports, the
pursuit of scientific discovery, active commitments to political or community affairs, or membership in a service
club.

Perhaps you are among the many who find life meaning
and purpose through religion. Increasing numbers of people
appear to be deciding that some sort of religious faith is
necessary if they are to find order and meaning in life.[10] Belief in God helps us make sense of the universe, find comfort in times of distress, and see meaning even when bad
things happen to good people.

An Ancient Example

Israel's King David had a life philosophy built around his
deep commitment to God. Author of some of the world's
best-loved religious literature, David freely shared his beliefs, hopes, discouragements, frustrations, fears, intellectual struggles, and joys. He admitted his weaknesses,
centuries before such openness was popular. When he fell
into sin, he confessed what he had done and experienced
forgiveness.

Read David's writings and life story, however, and you

will be impressed most with his view of God. Despite all his human weaknesses and pressures, David kept reminding himself what his God must be like. Consider, for example, the following excerpt from Psalms 145:3–8, 18, 19. It gives a clear basis for one man's life philosophy.

> Great is the Lord and most worthy of praise;
>   his greatness no one can fathom.
> One generation will commend your works to another;
>   they will tell of your mighty acts.
> They will speak of the glorious splendor of your majesty,
>   and I will meditate on your wonderful works.
> They will tell of the power of your awesome works,
>   and I will proclaim your great deeds.
> They will celebrate your abundant goodness
>   and joyfully sing of your righteousness.
> The Lord is gracious and compassionate,
>   slow to anger and rich in love. . . .
> The Lord is near to all who call on him,
>   to all who call on him in truth.
> He fulfills the desires of those who fear him;
>   he hears their cry and saves them.

A Small View of God

During World War II, a perceptive young pastor helped his London parishioners cope with the pressures of war by showing how the Bible is relevant to contemporary life. J. B. Phillips published a modern translation of the New Testament that eventually brought comfort and enlightenment to millions of readers around the world.

As he studied the sacred Book, Phillips was impressed with its ring of authenticity and its powerful view of God.[11] David thought that God was a Being who is big and powerful. In contrast, suggested J. B. Phillips, many modern people have a view of God that is small. They view Him as little more than a grandfatherly "man upstairs" or "elder brother in the sky" who isn't much aware of the contemporary complex world and isn't much inclined to get involved.

People with such views of God see no reason to give religion a prominent place in their life philosophies. A problem with many people today, writes Phillips, is that they

> ... have not found a God big enough for modern needs. While their experience of life has grown in a score of directions, and their mental horizons have been expanded to the point of bewilderment by world events and by scientific discoveries, their ideas of God have remained largely static. . . .
>
> There are undoubtedly professing Christians with childish conceptions of God which could not stand up to the winds of real life for five minutes. . . .
>
> Many men and women today are living, often with inner dissatisfaction, without any faith in God at all. This is not because they are particularly wicked or selfish or, as the old-fashioned would say, "godless," but because they have not found with their adult minds a God big enough to "account for" life, big enough to command their highest admiration and respect, and consequently their willing co-operation.[12]

The God of the Bible is no small creation of the human imagination. He is the kind of Being described by David; one who is big enough to sustain an ancient king, a group of Londoners during the bombings of World War II, a couple of North Americans in the heart of Africa, and more modern life managers, like you and me.

A Personal Faith

According to Ira Progoff, in Freud's Victorian era, the "awful secret nobody wanted to talk about was sex. Today, the awful secret is spirituality."[13] Many seem willing to talk about almost anything except their inner beliefs.

I saw this at a recent seminar on stress management. The instructor freely discussed every subject, but his discomfort and embarrassment was visible to everyone when he was asked about religion. Quickly he slithered over the topic and announced a coffee break when the questions kept coming. His was a dramatic illustration of our freedom and willingness to be open about sex, but our hesitations to deal head-on with religion.

I can respect those who view religious beliefs as a part of life that is intimate and deeply personal. In this culture nobody appreciates the fanatic who constantly tries to push his or her beliefs onto others. How you or I communicate with God can be a private matter.

Very often, however, the reluctance to talk about religion really hides an unwillingness to face and consider ultimate religious issues. Life can be empty when one ignores religion and pays little attention to developing a philosophy that goes beyond the pragmatic present. It is more honest and far healthier to consider what we believe and attempt to spell out our views of the universe.

What is your view of God? How do your beliefs influence your life and contribute to your self-management?

For me, strength and ultimate encouragement come from my convictions about the existence and influence of God. As a life philosophy, I try to follow the advice of King David's son who wrote, "In everything you do, put God first, and he will direct you . . ." (Proverbs 3:6 TLB). This is a life philosophy that involves:

Belief. This is more than a passing acknowledgment that God might be a possibility. It is belief in the existence of a big God who is alive and aware of the events and individuals in this universe. He is a God who "so loved the world that he gave his one and only Son, that whoever believes in him shall not perish but have eternal life" (John 3:16). According to the Bible, "If you confess with your mouth, 'Jesus is Lord,' and believe in your heart that God raised him from the dead, you will be saved" (Romans 10:9). Such beliefs do not guarantee a life that is easier, but a life that acknowledges Christ's lordship will be fulfilling (John 10:10).

Growth. As a psychologist and a writer, I constantly read the literature and seek to grow in my profession. The same is true of my spiritual life. Growth comes to those who feed their inner lives by prayer, times of worship, and input from the Scriptures and other religious literature. Like the baby who doesn't grow unless it eats, or the professional who stagnates when he or she fails to keep up-to-date, so the believer needs regular times for the intake of spiritual nourishment.

Obedience. Like soldiers under marching orders, true believers strive to obey the teachings of their God. "If you love me, you will obey what I command," Jesus told His followers. "Whoever has my commands and obeys them, he is the one who loves me . . ." (John 14:15, 21).

Spiritual Power. Read the New Testament Book of Acts and you will see a true story of persecution, struggle, and difficulties with life management. But the story is also one of joy, caring, and meaning. The story is a demonstration of God's power working through individual lives that had clear direction and purpose. From the time of Jesus down to the present, believers have known an underlying peace and power that brings comfort and inner security, especially in times of need. This is no irrelevant, pie-in-the-sky theory. For many, it forms the basis of their whole approach to life management.

To help you consider these issues as they relate to your own life philosophy, you may want to fill out the spiritual values questionnaire at the end of this chapter. Once again, there are no right or wrong answers; the questionnaire is designed to help you think through your own views.

Effective Life Management
Involves Forgiveness

I can still remember a conversation that occurred over thirty years go when I was a young psychology student, spending the summer at work in a state mental hospital. I was having coffee with a member of the hospital staff, a seasoned counselor who had given his life to help those in bondage to various forms of mental illness.

"The major problem with these people," he said, looking around the crowded room, "is their inability to forgive or to accept forgiveness. Religious and nonreligious people both need to experience forgiveness."[14]

Simon Wiesenthal was not a mental patient, but for a time he was imprisoned in the Mauthausen concentration camp in Poland. One day, when he was assigned to clean rubbish from a barn, his hard labor was interrupted by a nurse who took him to a young SS trooper.

The trooper, scarcely out of his teens, was clearly dying. His face was bandaged with pus-soaked rags; his eyes gazed from gray sockets almost hidden by dirty gauze; his voice was weak. Holding Wiesenthal's hand, the soldier said he had to talk to a Jew; he could not die until he had confessed the sins he had committed against helpless Jewish people. He told a story of incredible horror and cruelty, then asked the Jewish prisoner for forgiveness.

Wiesenthal listened silently without saying a word. Then, abruptly, he stood to his feet and walked briskly out of the room.

No word was spoken.

There was no forgiveness.

It is easy to be critical of this persecuted and unforgiving prisoner, but how would you have responded in similar circumstances? As he told this story many years later, Wie-

senthal was sure he had made the right decision.[15] To forgive, he said, would have been to admit that the Holocaust
was not evil.

To forgive is difficult, terribly difficult. It isn't fair. Why
should Wiesenthal forgive and let someone else off the
hook? Why, the former prisoner reasoned, should a man on
his deathbed be given a quick word of forgiveness for his
monumental acts of evil? In our period of history, long after
the horrors of Nazism, many would agree with the disgrun-
tled politician who recently stood before a bank of media
microphones and announced: "I don't get mad, but I'll get
even."

Why Forgive?

Dr. Hans Selye would disagree with this philosophy. The
famous stress researcher, who was mentioned in chapter 2,
concluded that revenge is the greatest possible threat to an
individual's security. Refusing to forgive and trying to get
even is natural, he admitted, but revenge "can only hurt
both the giver and the receiver of its fruits."[16]

Professor Lewis Smedes goes further and argues that revenge and a refusal to forgive can make life continually
miserable. The person who refuses to forgive is perpetually
frustrated, enslaved by thoughts of how to get even, never
free from the bitterness of the past. Forgiveness, writes
Smedes, brings relief and fairness to the forgiver.[17]

Is it fair to be stuck to a painful past? Is it fair to be wal-
loped again and again by the old unfair hurt? Vengeance is
having a videotape planted in your soul that cannot be
turned off. It plays the painful scene over and over again inside your mind. It hooks you into its instant replays. And
each time it replays, you feel the clap of pain again. Is this
fair?

Forgiving turns off the videotape of pained memory. Forgiving sets you free.

It takes time to really forgive. It takes courage and it may be a long time before you forget—if ever.

The person who forgives does not try to pretend that suffering and injustice never existed. Forgiveness is not smoothing things over and putting on a happy face. When we forgive there is no guarantee that the forgiven person will change, confess to wrongdoing, or even accept our forgiveness. Judeo-Christian religion believes that justice will ultimately be done, but this may not occur during our lifetimes.[18]

Forgiveness is the only way to set yourself free from a painful past. Selye's words are difficult to follow but deeply insightful: "No sane person would consciously select the savage satisfactions of the vendetta as an ultimate aim in life."[19] Is that what the counselor at the mental hospital was saying so many years ago?

Effective life managers learn to forgive.

They also accept forgiveness.

Accepting Forgiveness

This is one unique feature of Christianity. Jesus Christ forgives—unconditionally and without demanding restitution. "If we claim to be without sin, we deceive ourselves and the truth is not in us. If we confess our sins, he is faithful and just and will forgive us our sins and purify us from all unrighteousness" (1 John 1:8, 9). Others may not forgive us, but God does. We may have trouble forgiving ourselves, but God has no trouble forgiving freely.

There isn't much we can do to change a painful past. To ruminate is to stay tied to previous experiences. To forgive and accept forgiveness is to start over and move on into the future. That is powerfully effective life management.

> **Effective Life Management Involves
> Contact With Others**

If you wander into the self-help section of a local bookstore or library, you are likely to find shelves of books that present variations of one basic message—life depends on you. You are urged to control your passages through life, take care of your erroneous zones, look out for number one, win over worry, manage your money, close the sale, make a habit of success, develop the power of positive thinking, win friends and influence people.

To some extent this is the American way and it isn't all bad. The rugged individualism and pioneer spirit that permeated the life of Otto Keller has motivated thousands to overcome obstacles, accomplish feats of greatness, and manage lives effectively.

But no person is an island and only fools try to succeed on their own.

Carroll O'Connor is no fool. Known around the world as television's Archie Bunker, he was seen regularly by 50 million people when "All in the Family" was at its height of popularity. The actor who played Archie Bunker is really a soft-spoken, articulate gentleman who comes from a family of teachers and who almost returned to the classroom when he failed repeatedly to find acting jobs in the 1950s.

What was the worst thing he faced at the struggling start of his career?

"Rejection," O'Connor replied in a recent interview.[20] It lasted for years and led to frustration, discouragement, and sometimes bitterness.

It's impossible to be an actor by yourself. Agents, reviewers, critics, fellow actors, and the all-important audience must be part of the actor's life. Unlike some of his successful colleagues who are cocky and aloof from people,

Carroll O'Connor still tries to be sensitive to others and gracious to his fans.

Is this a reminder for those of us who never appear on television and will never set foot on a stage? All the world is a stage, said Shakespeare. We who try to manage our life performances from day to day cannot ignore other people.

Reach Out and Touch Someone

Within recent years, psychologists have emphasized the importance of what they call mutual support networks. Each of us needs other people—family, friends, neighbors, colleagues, fellow believers—to give guidance, strength, help, support, friendship, fun, and encouragement. In a dog-eat-dog, me-first environment, nobody wins; eventually everybody loses. When there is mutual support and caring, we all benefit.

There is much we can do alone in this life. Religious people often pray, meditate, worship, and read sacred literature by themselves. But no healthy person withdraws completely. Over fifty times, the New Testament writers use the words *one another*. Believers were encouraged to care for one another, be kind to one another, help one another, serve one another, be patient with one another, pray for one another, live in peace with one another, build up one another, and encourage one another.

Some time ago, the telephone company encouraged us to reach out and touch someone. Reaching out and caring is the essence of practical religion. Jesus told the disciples to let love be their most obvious characteristic (John 13:34, 35). One of the apostles described the truly religious person as one who avoided gossip, kept away from the world's pollution, and cared for those people who couldn't care for themselves (James 1:26, 27).

People who reach out and care for others are individuals

who find meaning in life and escape from the traps of lone-liness and self-centered approaches to life management.

Some would say the suggestion is radical, but ultimate life management involves continual close contact with other people and a willingness to care.

Effective Life Management Is Risky

The Scott Meredith Literary Agency in Manhattan has represented some of the biggest names in modern writing. Norman Mailer, Carl Sagan, Margaret Truman, Gary Wills, Elliott Roosevelt, and a host of others have leaned on the expertise of Scott Meredith and the staff of his immensely successful agency.

"What would you suggest to someone who really wants to change his life?" Mr. Meredith was asked recently.

"First," he replied, "I'd ask, 'Are you willing to take a risk?' I'd explain that not one of the talented people I've known has been truly confident, particularly when chang-ing his or her life. . . . We can always find very good, per-suasive reasons not to do something." That, added Scott Meredith, is why many people never start new careers or begin new lives. They are unwilling to take the risk.[21]

Oysters and Eagles

I once heard a speaker draw a contrast between oysters and eagles. The oyster, he suggested, is a symbol of secu-rity. It remains in its shell and rarely ventures into areas that are dangerous or unknown.

Baby eagles try to do the same. They are hatched in a nest that surrounds them with protection from the wind, is lined with warm feathers and stays securely anchored to a ledge

well above the dangers of the valleys below. Maybe the ea-
glets would like to remain in the comforts of the nest, but
they don't have that choice. The day comes when they are
pushed out. Sometimes they fall hundreds of feet before the
parent eagle swoops them up—and pushes them out again.
Before an eagle can soar, it has to risk falling.

Isn't this true of us as well?

Ricky Hosea took a risk when he determined to walk out
of that rehabilitation center. Steve and Phil Mahre took
risks when they tore down that Yugoslavian mountain in
the winter Olympics. Bernie, whose men's store went out of
business, took a risk, and so did Father Ritter when he re-
signed his comfortable teaching job and went to work with
those sex-exploited kids in New York. And what about
Robin Graham who sailed around the world, John Ehrlichman who chose life instead of suicide, Kevin Robinson who
writes novels with one finger, old John Stennis who looks
ahead rather than backward, Norman Cousins who refused
to be stopped by terminal illness, the little band of performers in the Culpepper and Merriweather Great Combined Circus, Corrie ten Boom who forgave her Nazi
tormentor, Charles Colson who works in prisons, Dr. Nick
Stinnett who works at saving families, Shirley Jones who
raised a show-business family, Sister Ryan who made the
Navajos her family, Madelon DeVoe Talley and Lee Iacocca
who got fired, Louisa May Alcott who gave her life for
others, F. W. Woolworth who quit the hardware store so he
could make a fortune, Piet Derksen who gave away his fortune, Jack Levering who published his own book, and Otto
Keller who had no time to write books? This is a diverse
group of ordinary people who got their lives out of neutral
by daring to take risks.

A few of them did it alone. Most had help from their
friends. Several saw the hand of God guiding their lives.

Holding It All Together

There was, among them, the young man who started drinking to escape the feelings of emptiness and despondency. At first there was only a cocktail or two, but soon he was drinking more and more. He got into drugs, attempted to escape by partying, and wrecked his brand-new car while trying to drive home through an alcoholic haze.

"I was overwhelmed by guilt and shame," he wrote later.

"When I was alone, a wave of depression moved in on me like a cold fog rolling in off the sea. I reached for a wine bottle."

That night, the young man decided he was a failure. His wife and child, he concluded, would be better without him. Taking a gun from its hiding place, he staggered to his feet and stepped outside into the fresh air.

> Through bloodshot eyes I looked, so I believed, for the last time at those whom I loved so much. . . .
>
> It is hard to know if I seriously considered putting the gun to my head and my finger to the trigger. What I do remember is hearing quick, fast footsteps behind me before Patti grabbed the gun and, in one continuous movement, tossed it into the water.[22]

Robin Graham, the boy who sailed around the world alone, might have killed himself if his young wife hadn't tossed that gun into the oily waters of the marina.

But God had other plans. Standing a few weeks later on a mountain pass in Idaho, Robin took Patti's hand and did something he hadn't done for a long time.

He prayed.

"Lord Jesus, take care of the three of us. Show us where You want us to go. Show us what You want us to do. Please forgive us for all the wrong things we have done. Help us to understand Your teaching in the Bible. Give us the courage to obey You. From this day on we give You control of our lives."

The young couple was overwhelmed by a feeling of freedom. It was like a great boulder had fallen from their shoulders and rolled down the mountain.

They got back into their van and drove off. From that time they had a new faith to hold their lives together. From that time they learned what it can be like to manage life with an outside source of guidance.

Spiritual Values Questionnaire

Beliefs: If somebody asked you what you really believe about God and the universe, what would you say? This is a difficult question, but please try to write your three most important beliefs. Use more paper if necessary.

1. _____

_____

2. _____

_____

3. _____

_____

Actions: What do you do differently in your life because of your beliefs? (Some Christians pray, for example. Some people give part of their money to charity or to the church. Some people have lifestyles or views about sex or money that reflect their beliefs.) What, if anything, is different about your life because of what you believe? Try to be honest. Use extra paper if you need more space.

1. _____

_____

2. _____

_____

3. _____

_____

There is clear evidence that people who have some kind of religious faith handle stress and manage their lives better. The Bible states, however, that faith is worthless and dead if it doesn't influence our lives and make a difference in the way we live. Is your faith dead or alive?

Is yours a casual religion or one that makes a difference in the way you live? Discuss this with a friend.

At some time you may want to look up the following Bible verses. How do they apply to you?

John 3:16; 1 John 1:8, 9; John 13:34, 35; John 14:15

Source
Notes

Chapter 1: Managing Your Life

1. Ann Marie Lipinski, "A Long Walk Back," *Chicago Tribune*, February 8, 1985. In preparing this section, I have drawn on this moving and skillfully written newspaper article. I am grateful to Mr. Hosea for allowing me to tell his story.

2. M. Scott Peck, *The Road Less Traveled* (New York: Simon and Schuster / Touchstone, 1978).

3. A partial listing of these authors and their works appears in the bibliography of this book, page 237.

4. Gary Emery, *Own Your Own Life* (New York: New American Library/Signet, 1982).

5. Ibid., pp. 12–15.

6. Gordon MacDonald, *Ordering Your Private World* (Nashville: Thomas Nelson, 1984).

7. Howard Rutledge and Phyllis Rutledge with Mel White and Lyla White, *In the Presence of Mine Enemies* (Old Tappan, N.J.: Fleming H. Revell, 1973).

8. According to Howard Clinebell, Jr., this prayer has been attributed to "nearly every saint and seer in history" but eventually was traced to theologian Reinhold Niebuhr. Niebuhr, himself, isn't sure who wrote it. *See* Howard J. Clinebell, Jr., *Understanding and Counseling the Alcoholic*, rev. ed. (Nashville: Abingdon, 1968), pp. 152, 153.

9. Research in support of this conclusion is summarized in chapter 1 of Robert L. Williams and James D. Long, *Toward a Self-Managed Life-Style*, 3d ed. (Boston: Houghton Mifflin, 1983).

10. Thomas J. Peters and Robert H. Waterman, Jr., *In Search of Excellence* (New York: Harper & Row, 1982); and Thomas J. Peters and Nancy K. Austin, *A Passion for Excellence* (New York: Random House, 1985).

11. Tom Peters, "What Price Success? Think About It," *Chicago Tribune*, August 26, 1985.

12. *See*, for example, R. M. Eisler and L. W. Frederiksen, *Perfecting Social Skills: A Guide to Interpersonal Behavior Development* (New York: Plenum, 1980).

13. Denis Waitley, *The Double Win* (Old Tappan, N.J.: Fleming H. Revell, 1985).

14. Psychiatrist William Glasser used these words to title a book on life management. William Glasser, *Take Effective Control of Your Life* (New York: Harper & Row, 1984).

Chapter 2: Managing Your Stress

1. The term was suggested by Colonel Russell V. Ritchey, founder of Squadron Officer School at the USAF Air University, Maxwell Air Force Base, Alabama.

2. This three-fold classification has been suggested by Dr. George Pollack, former president of the Chicago Insti-

tute for Psychotherapy and professor of psychology and behavioral science at Northwestern University Medical School. *See* Sallie Gaines, "Managing Exec Stress," *Chicago Tribune*, August 18, 1985.

3. At the turn of the century, there was great debate about whether evaluation comes before or after the physiological response. Perhaps it doesn't make much difference since both occur almost simultaneously.

4. Hans Selye, *The Stress of Life* (New York: McGraw-Hill, 1956), p. 285.

5. Selye, *Stress of Life*, p. 284, italics added.

6. Meyer Friedman and Ray H. Rosenman, *Type A Behavior and Your Heart* (New York: Alfred A. Knopf, 1974).

7. Karl Albrecht, *Stress and the Manager* (Englewood Cliffs, N.J.: Prentice-Hall, 1979).

8. It should be added that recent research has shown that some intense anxiety may also have a clear physical cause. *See* David V. Sheehan, *The Anxiety Disease* (New York: Charles Scribner's Sons, 1983).

9. John D. Adams, ed., *Understanding and Managing Stress: A Book of Readings* (San Diego: University Associates, 1980). *See* page 204.

10. Meyer Friedman and Diane Ulmer, *Treating Type A Behavior and Your Heart* (New York: Alfred A. Knopf, 1984).

11. The study was conducted by Dr. Lester Breslow, dean of UCLA's School of Public Medicine. Reported in John D. Adams, *Understanding and Managing Stress*, pp. 24, 25.

Chapter 3: Managing Your Emotions

1. John G. Hubbell, "Father Ritter's Covenant," *Reader's Digest*, October 1980, pp. 116–120.

2. Tax-free contributions can be sent to Covenant House, 460 West 41 Street, New York, N.Y. 10036.

3. Quoted in Hubbell, "Father Ritter's Covenant."

4. Archibald D. Hart, *Feeling Free* (Old Tappan, N.J.: Fleming H. Revell, 1979).

5. John Leo, "Not by Issues Alone," *Time*, November 12, 1984, p. 37.

6. For example, *see* Robin Graham and Derek Gill, *The Boy Who Sailed 'Round the World Alone* (Waco: Word, 1985).

7. Ibid., p. 45.

8. John Carey with Mary Bruno, "Why Cynicism Can Be Fatal," *Newsweek*, September 10, 1984.

9. Michael G. Perri and C. Steven Richards, "An Investigation of Naturally Occurring Episodes of Self-Controlled Behaviors," *Journal of Counseling Psychology*, vol. 24, 1977, pp. 178–183.

10. Walter Anderson, *Courage Is a Three Letter Word* (New York: Random House, 1986), p. 5, italics added.

11. For further discussion of this, see my book, *The Magnificent Mind* (Waco: Word, 1985). *See also* Archibald D. Hart, *Adrenalin and Stress* (Waco: Word, 1986).

12. This research is summarized and the issue is discussed further by Carol Tavris, *Anger: The Misunderstood Emotion* (New York: Simon & Schuster / Touchstone, 1982).

13. Gary R. Collins, *Overcoming Anxiety* (Ventura, Calif.: Regal, 1973).

14. Gary Emery, *Own Your Own Life* (New York: Signet, 1982), pp. 156–158.

15. The term was used by Archibald D. Hart in *Feeling Free*.

16. Michael Hall, *Emotions: Sometimes I have them/Sometimes they have me* (St. Louis: Good-News Encounters, 1985). Available from 1333 N. 23rd Street, Grand Junction, CO. 81501.

Chapter 4: Managing Your Attitudes

1. Andrea Warren, "One Letter At a Time," *Writer's Digest*, June 1985, pp. 6, 7.

2. Dale E. Galloway, *Twelve Ways to Develop a Positive Attitude* (Wheaton: Tyndale, 1975), p. 25.

3. Kenneth R. Pelletier, *Mind as Healer; Mind as Slayer* (New York: Dell/Delta Book, 1977).

4. Norman Cousins describes his experiences in *Anatomy of an Illness* (New York: Norton, 1979). The wise man is King Solomon whose words are recorded in the Bible.

5. Norman Cousins, *The Healing Heart* (New York: Norton, 1983).

6. I am grateful to my colleague, Dr. William Secor, for this paraphrase which he enjoys quoting to his students and to me, whenever I have problems with a lack of writing motivation.

7. These are described in more detail in Dr. Garfield's books. For an excellent overview of his conclusions *see* Charles Garfield, *Peak Performers: The New Heroes of American Business* (New York: William Morrow, 1986).

8. Galloway, *Twelve Ways*, pp. 31–40. In the following paragraphs, I have rephrased and condensed Galloway's "Twelve ways you can eliminate the negative and activate the positive."

Chapter 5: Managing Your Relationships

1. This description of the Culpepper and Merriweather Great Combined Circus is adapted from Ron Grossman, "The Smallest Show on Earth," *Chicago Tribune*, July 10, 1986.

2. Some of the material from the following paragraphs is adapted from my book *Living in Peace: The Psychology of Interpersonal Relations*. Published in 1970 by a now defunct publisher, the book has been out of print for several years.

3. From Erich Fromm, *The Sane Society* (New York: Rinehart, 1955), p. 4.

4. Tim Stafford, *The Friendship Gap: Reaching Out Across Cultures* (Downers Grove, Ill.: InterVarsity, 1984), p. 25.

5. Bibb Lanane and John M. Darley, *The Unresponsive Bystander: Why Doesn't He Help?* (New York: Appleton-Century-Crofts, 1970).

6. These views are summarized by Stevenson Swanson, "Leading Question: What Kind of People Do Others Follow?" *Chicago Tribune,* November 29, 1984. Warren Bennis has summarized his conclusions in a book: Warren Bennis and Burt Nanus, *Leaders: The Strategies for Taking Charge* (New York: Harper & Row, 1985).

7. Bob Greene, "Childhood Cruelties Last for Generations," *Chicago Tribune,* December 30, 1985.

Chapter 6: Managing Your Family

1. The following quotation is taken from Dr. Stinnett's address to a national conference on family building held in Washington, D.C., during the summer of 1984. *See* Nick Stinnett, "Six Qualities That Make a Family Strong" in George Rekers, ed., *Family Building: Six Qualities of a Strong Family* (Ventura, Calif.: Regal, 1985), p. 36. The Rekers volume includes all of the major addresses given at the Washington conference.

2. David R. Mace, "Strictly Personal: Expressing Affection in Families," *Marriage and Family Living,* November 1980.

3. Dolores Curran, *Traits of a Healthy Family* (New York: Harper & Row, 1983), p. 59.

4. Ibid., p. 61.

5. The following is adapted from Gary R. Collins, "How Expressing Appreciation in Families Can Help Prevent Problems," in George Rekers, ed., *Family Building,* pp. 281–292.

6. John Q. Baucom, *Fatal Choice: The Teenage Suicide Crisis* (Chicago: Moody Press, 1986).

7. Ron Lee Davis, *Gold in the Making* (Nashville: Thomas Nelson, 1983).

8. Nick Stinnett, et al., "How Strong Families Cope With Crises," *Family Perspectives*, vol. 15, 1981, pp. 159–166.

9. Pat and Jill Williams, with Jerry Jenkins, *Rekindled* (Old Tappan, N.J.: Fleming H. Revell, 1985).

Chapter 7: Managing Your Career

1. Robert Kerwin, "Musings of a Show-biz Matriarch," *Chicago Tribune Magazine*, May 13, 1979.

2. Gordon MacDonald, *Ordering Your Private World* (Nashville: Thomas Nelson, 1984).

3. Muriel Dobbin, "Is the Daily Grind Wearing You Down?" *U.S. News & World Report*, March 24, 1986.

4. Brad Patten, "Clinic Provides Strong Medicine," *Chicago Tribune*, July 28, 1986. The story first appeared in the *Phoenix Gazette*.

5. Kerwin, "Musings of a Show-biz Matriarch."

6. Eric Berne, *Games People Play* (New York: Grove Press, 1964).

7. From an interview in *Writer's Digest*, September 1986, p. 7.

8. This story was told as part of an article by Joan L. Guest, "We Are Driven: The Success Syndrome and How It Affects You," *His*, vol. 49, October 1979.

9. Denis Waitley, *Seeds of Greatness* (Old Tappan, N.J.: Fleming H. Revell, 1983), p. 189.

10. Fran Tarkenton, "Tarkenton on Management: Job Satisfaction: The Popular Myth, the Unpopular Reality," *Sky*, vol. 8, August 1979, pp. 34–36. Italics added.

11. Charles Garfield, *Peak Performers: The New Heroes of American Business* (New York: William Morrow, 1986), p. 266.

12. Madelon DeVoe Talley, *Career Hang Gliding: A Per-*

sonal Guide to Managing Your Career (New York: Dutton, 1986).

13. Art Spikol, "For Love and Money," *Writer's Digest,* February 1985, p. 48.

14. Paul Darcy Boles, "Changing Styles," *Writer's Digest,* April 1985, p. 27.

15. Talley, *Career Hang Gliding,* p. 294.

16. Brian T. Yates, *Self-Management: The Science and Art of Helping Yourself* (Belmont, Calif.: Wadsworth, 1985), p. 327.

17. Bruce A. Baldwin, "Decontaminating Your Leisure: Cornerstone of Lifestyle Management," *Pace,* vol. 9, September/October 1982.

18. Ibid.

Chapter 8: Managing Your Resources

1. *U.S. News & World Report,* March 24, 1986, pp. 65–69.

2. The idea of a money autobiography came to my attention in a short article by Catherine Snow, "Discover Your Feelings About Money," *Family Life Today,* vol. 11, April 1985, p. 22.

3. Reported by Robert Banks, *The Tyranny of Time: When 24 Hours Is Not Enough* (Downers Grove, Ill.: InterVarsity, 1983), p. 18.

4. Ibid.

5. Richard Eisner and Brett James, "Inside the Financial-planning Game: How Planners Can Help, How They Can Hurt," *Bottom Line Personal,* May 15, 1985, pp. 5, 6.

6. Alfred Goodloe, Jane Bensahel, and John Kelly, *Managing Yourself: How to Control Emotion, Stress, and Time* (New York: Franklin Watts, 1984).

7. Charles E. Hummel, *The Tyranny of the Urgent* (Downers Grove, Ill.: InterVarsity, 1967).

Chapter 9: Managing Your Self

1. Ronald Klug, *How to Keep a Spiritual Journal* (Nashville: Thomas Nelson, 1982), p. 9.

2. Ira Progoff, *At a Journal Workshop: The Basic Text and Guide for Using the 'Intensive Journal' Process* (New York: Dialogue House, 1975).

3. Ibid., p. 20.

4. Ruth Vaughn, *Write to Discover Yourself* (Garden City, N.Y.: Doubleday-Galilee, 1980).

5. Sidney M. Jourard, *The Transparent Self,* rev. ed. (New York: Van Nostrand Reinhold, 1971), p. 6.

6. Ibid., p. 7.

7. Kenneth Vaux, "How Do I Love Me?" *Christianity Today,* September 20, 1985, pp. 23–26. The following classification of attitudes is built on Professor Vaux's thoughtful article.

8. *Seven Winning Ways to Fight Cancer,* distributed by Lake Forest Hospital, Lake Forest, Illinois, n.d.

9. Ibid.

10. This information is adapted from information supplied by the University of Iowa School of Dentistry.

11. Quoted in Kenneth R. Pelletier, *Healthy People in Unhealthy Places: Stress and Fitness at Work* (New York: A Merloyd Lawrence Book, 1984), p. 1.

12. Ibid.

13. Marilee Horton and Walter Byrd, *Keeping Your Balance* (Waco: Word, 1984), p. 47.

14. Ibid.

15. "New Rules of Exercise," *U.S. News & World Report,* August 11, 1986, p. 52.

16. American Medical Association, *Guide to Better Sleep* (New York: Random House).

17. Cited in Ray Hodgson and Peter Miller, *Self-Watching: Addictions, Habits, Compulsions: What to Do About Them* (New York: Facts on File, 1982), p. 11.

18. The following few paragraphs are adapted from Hodgson and Miller, *Self-Watching*.

19. Denis Waitley, *Seeds of Greatness* (Old Tappan, N.J.: Fleming H. Revell, 1983), p. 148.

20. Reported by Eric Zorn, "Retiree Buys Immortality in Hardcover," *Chicago Tribune*, August 8, 1986. The book by Jack Levering is titled *Out of the Night, Into the Wind* (New York: Vantage Press), 1986.

21. Leon Martel, *Mastering Change* (New York: Simon and Schuster, 1986).

22. "Viewpoint: Dr. Leon Martel. How to Profit from Change," *For Members Only: A Newsletter for American Express Cardholders*, April 1986.

Chapter 10: Managing Your Destiny

1. W. Phillip Keller, "Otto C. Keller," in Charles Turner, ed., *Chosen Vessels: Portraits of Ten Outstanding Christian Men* (Ann Arbor: Vine Books [Servant Publications] 1985), pp. 93, 92, 95, and 99.

2. Ibid., p. 104.

3. Ibid., p. 97.

4. Viktor Frankl, *The Unheard Cry for Meaning* (New York: Bantam, 1978).

5. Cited by I. D. Yalom, *Existential Psychotherapy* (New York: Basic Books, 1980).

6. Ibid., p. 423.

7. Viktor Frankl, *Man's Search for Meaning* (New York: Washington Square Press, 1963).

8. This summary is adapted from Yalom, *Existential Psychotherapy*.

9. Gerald Corey, *I Never Knew I Had a Choice*, 3d ed. (Monterey: Brooks/Cole, 1986), p. 346.

10. Ibid.

11. J. B. Phillips, *Ring of Truth: A Translator's Testimony* (New York: Macmillan, 1967).

12. J. B. Phillips, *Your God Is Too Small* (London: Epworth Press, 1982). The quotation is taken from pages 7 and 8.

13. Robert Blair Kaiser, "The Way of the Journal," *Psychology Today*, March 1981, p. 74.

14. I apologize to readers who have seen this example in an earlier book. In my opinion, it is important enough that it bears repeating.

15. Simon Wiesenthal, *The Sunflower* (New York: Shocken, 1976).

16. Hans Selye, *The Stress of Life* (New York: McGraw-Hill, 1956), p. 286.

17. Lewis B. Smedes, "Forgiveness: The Power to Change the Past," *Christianity Today*, January 7, 1983, pp. 22–26.

18. *See* Psalm 73, for example.

19. Selye, *Stress of Life*, p. 286.

20. Walter Anderson, *Courage Is a Three Letter Word* (New York: Random House, 1986), p. 203.

21. Ibid., pp. 220, 221.

22. Robin Graham and Derek Gill, *The Boy Who Sailed 'Round the World Alone* (Waco: Word, 1985), p. 154.

Suggestions for Further Reading

The following books deal in some way with life management. They are among those the author consulted in preparing this book. A brief sentence or two has been added to describe the books you might find most helpful.

Alexander, Joe. *Dare to Change: How to Program Yourself for Success.* New York: Signet (New American Library), 1984.

Anderson, Walter. *Courage Is a Three Letter Word.* New York: Random House, 1986.

The "three-letter word" is *yes*—and the book is excellent. Written in a captivating style, the author gives guidance and success stories from famous personalities who had the courage to overcome fears.

Banks, Robert. *The Tyranny of Time: When 24 Hours Is Not Enough.* Downers Grove, Ill.: InterVarsity, 1983.

Bolton, Robert. *People Skills: How to Assert Yourself, Listen to Others, and Resolve Conflicts.* Englewood Cliffs, N.J.: Prentice-Hall, 1979.

Collins, Gary R. *Getting Started: Direction for the Most Important Decisions in Life.* Old Tappan, N.J.: Fleming H. Revell, 1984.

Written primarily for readers in their twenties and thirties, this book gives practical guidance for handling independence, marriage, singleness, parenthood, career planning, and other decisions of young adulthood.

Collins, Gary R. *The Magnificent Mind.* Waco: Word, 1985.

Not written as a life-management book, this still has a number of practical and entertaining ideas about stress, emotions, anxiety, maturity, creativity, dreaming, hypnosis, meditation, and similar subjects.

Corey, Gerald. *I Never Knew I Had a Choice,* 3d ed. Monterey: Brooks/Cole, 1986.

This was written as a college textbook and a personal workbook. It has in-depth, thought-provoking discussion on sex, your body, intimacy, solitude, work, meaning, values, and related issues.

Curran, Dolores. *Traits of a Healthy Family.* New York: Harper & Row, 1983.

George Gallup calls this "must reading for parents and young people." Based on a survey of people who work with families, this book describes fifteen traits often found in healthy families.

Douglass, Stephen B. *Managing Yourself: Practical Help for Christians in Personal Planning, Time Scheduling and Self-Control.* San Bernardino: Here's Life Publishers, 1978.

Emery, Gary. *Own Your Own Life: How the New Cognitive Therapy Can Make You Feel Wonderful.* New York: Signet (New American Library), 1982.

Executive Fitness Newsletter. *Fifty Ways to Stay Fit on a Busy Schedule.* Emmaus, Pa.: Rodale, 1980.

Garfield, Charles. *Peak Performers: The New Heroes of American Business.* New York: Morrow, 1986.

This is a fascinating, well-written discussion of attributes that lead some people to be successful peak performers. Highly recommended.

Glass, Bill. *Expect to Win.* Waco: Word, 1981.

Glasser, William. *Take Effective Control of Your Life.* New York: Harper & Row, 1984.

Goodloe, Alfred; Bensahel, Jane; and Kelly, John. *Managing Yourself: How to Control Emotion, Stress, and Time.* New York: Watts, 1986.

Hart, Archibald. *Feeling Free: Effective Ways to Make Your Emotions Work for You.* Old Tappan, N.J.: Fleming H. Revell, 1979.

This is a well-written and potentially liberating discussion of emotions, with specific discussions of anger, depression, self-hate, guilt, and love. Worth reading.

Hart, Archibald. *The Hidden Link Between Adrenalin & Stress: The Exciting New Breakthrough That Helps You Overcome Stress Damage.* Word: Waco, 1986.

Hodgson, Ray, and Miller, Peter. *Self-Watching: Addictions, Habits, Compulsions: What to Do About Them.* New York: Facts on File, 1982.

This book may be difficult to find but it is worth getting. A well-written, practical volume dealing with issues such as anxiety, depression, overeating, smoking, workaholism, and a variety of compulsions. Illustrated with photographs.

Kassorla, Irene C. *Go For It! How To Win at Love, Work and Play.* New York: Dell, 1984.

MacDonald, Gordon. *Ordering Your Private World.* Nashville: Oliver-Nelson, 1984.

Written from a strong Christian perspective, this excellent volume is worth reading by anyone who wants to reappraise a frantic life-style or work on inner priorities. Widely acclaimed.

Mallough, Don. *You Can Manage Your Life.* Grand Rapids: Baker, 1981.

Martin, Robert A., and Poland, Elizabeth Y. *Learning to Change: A Self-Management Approach to Adjustment.* New York: McGraw-Hill, 1980.

McLemore, Clinton W. *Good Guys Finish First: Success Strategies for Business Men and Women.* New York: Jove, 1984.

McMinn, Gordon. *Choosing to Be Close: Fill Your Life With Rewarding Relationships.* Portland: Multnomah, 1984.

Newman, Mildred, and Berkowitz, Bernard. *How to Take Charge of Your Life.* New York: Harcourt Brace Jovanovich, 1977.

Ogilvie, Lloyd J. *Making Stress Work for You: Ten Proven Principles.* Waco: Word, 1984.

Schuller, Robert H. *Tough Times Never Last, But Tough People Do!* New York: Bantam, 1983.

Slocum, Robert E. *Ordinary Christians in a High-Tech World.* Waco: Word, 1986.

Talley, Madelon DeVoe. *Career Hang Gliding: A Personal Guide to Managing Your Career.* New York: Dutton, 1986.

A fascinating and personal reflection from a lady who shares her ups and downs working in the corporate business world. Readable and practical.

Waitley, Denis. *The Double Win.* Old Tappan, N.J.: Fleming H. Revell, 1985.

A motivation expert shares ways to excel in life while you help others win as well. Worth reading.

Waitley, Denis. *Seeds of Greatness: The Ten Best-Kept Secrets of Total Success.* Old Tappan, N.J.: Fleming H. Revell, 1983.

This is a practical, well-written, and inspiring book that could be of help and interest to anyone who wants to manage life more effectively. Highly recommended.

Watson, David L., and Tharp, Roland G. *Self-Directed Behavior: Self-Modification for Personal Adjustment,* 3d ed. Monterey: Brooks/Cole, 1981.

Wheat, Ed and Gaye. *Intended for Pleasure: Sex Technique and Sexual Fulfillment in Christian Marriage.* Old Tappan, N.J.: Fleming H. Revell, 1977.

This is a practical, illustrated, tastefully written guide by a physician and his wife. One of the finest on this topic.

Wheeler, David R. *Control Yourself.* Chicago: Nelson-Hall, 1976.

Williams, Robert L., and Long, James D. *Toward a Self-Managed Life-Style,* 3d ed. Boston: Houghton-Mifflin, 1983.

Wilson, Earl D. *The Discovered Self: The Search for Self-Acceptance.* Downers Grove, Ill.: InterVarsity, 1985.

Yates, Brian Y. *Self-Management: The Science and Art of Helping Yourself.* Belmont, Calif.: Wadsworth, 1985.

Index